SEX
SIGNS

SEX
SIGNS

Your Perfect Match Is in the Stars

Constance Stellas

ADAMS MEDIA

NEW YORK LONDON TORONTO SYDNEY NEW DELHI

Adams Media
An Imprint of Simon & Schuster, Inc.
57 Littlefield Street
Avon, Massachusetts 02322

First Adams Media hardcover edition December 2018

ADAMS MEDIA and colophon are trademarks of Simon & Schuster.

For information about special discounts for bulk purchases, please contact Simon & Schuster Special Sales at 1-866-506-1949 or business@simonandschuster.com.

The Simon & Schuster Speakers Bureau can bring authors to your live event. For more information or to book an event contact the Simon & Schuster Speakers Bureau at 1-866-248-3049 or visit our website at www.simonspeakers.com.

Interior design by Sylvia McArdle

Manufactured in the United States of America

10 9 8 7 6 5 4 3 2 1

Library of Congress Cataloging-in-Publication Data has been applied for.

ISBN 978-1-5072-0948-6
ISBN 978-1-5072-0949-3 (ebook)

Contains material adapted from the following title published by Adams Media, an Imprint of Simon & Schuster, Inc.: *The Everything® Sex Signs Book, 2nd Edition* by Constance Stellas, copyright © 2011, ISBN 978-1-4405-1099-1.

Contents

Introduction

Sexual chemistry is mysterious. We can't always explain why we desire someone or feel a ping of attraction. This feeling bypasses our brains, makes us feel alive, and enhances all human communication. Sex can mark the beginning of a romance, a marriage, or an outrageous fling. There is just some special tingle between you and that person that only one thing, sex, will satisfy. Sometimes, one person has the feeling initially and the other doesn't. Not to worry—with a little effort and this handy book, you will be prepared to do everything possible to encourage a sexy relationship and get to know your own sexual personality.

There is a lot of sexual posturing in the media today, and a great deal of talk about who is sexy and who is not. Sex sells cars and clothing, and in the movies we are titillated by passion. The media give us lots of images and sexy ideas, but these images may not reflect our own sexual personalities, which are as individual and varied as other parts of our personalities. Astrology is one of the finest ways of investigating the unique currents of energy and desire that influence a person's sexuality. Understanding your partner's Sun sign gives you a personal sex manual to guide you toward what you will both enjoy.

As you read this book, you will begin to appreciate the myriad ways people express themselves. The "Hot and Not-So-Hot Combinations" sections deal with the archetypes of astrology. Many "not-so-hot" matches, or traditionally challenging combinations, have enjoyed great flings or long relationships. If you find that you are attracted to someone who doesn't rate according to the good matches, follow your own instincts, heart, and libido. The description of these matches is intended to give you a guideline, not permission or denial of permission. Sexual chemistry is, after all, somewhat unfathomable.

As you read this book, you will notice that each sign has several aspects. A sign has a gender (male or female) and an element (water, fire, air, or earth). All the water and earth signs are considered female, and all the air and fire signs are considered male. In addition to its element, each sign is categorized as one of three qualities: cardinal, fixed, or mutable. The cardinal signs initiate and lead each season; the fixed signs reign when the season is well established; and the mutable signs are changeable, partaking of one season and moving into the next one. Finally, each sign has a ruling planet that exemplifies the characteristics of the sign.

The two astrological planets that most concern sexual appetites, desires, and styles are Venus and Mars. Venus, or Aphrodite in ancient Greek mythology, was the goddess of beauty and erotic love. Mars, or Ares, was the god of war. All people have Venus and Mars located in a sign in their charts, and the placement of Mars and Venus will describe the yin and yang, or receptive and assertive, dynamic in their lives. The placement of Venus and Mars has nothing to do with traditional gender roles, as a man can be very yin and receptive, and a woman very yang and assertive.

Sex requires two to tango, and the insights in *Sex Signs* were written for both you and your partner. Whether you are the pursuer or the pursued, getting to know your sex sign profile will encourage you and your partner to communicate in the most delightful and intimate way possible. Don't think too much. Read this book, feel, and explore. It will bring smiles to you and your partner.

Sex Signs
Compatibility Quiz

The following compatibility quiz will help you find a new way to look at yourself and your partner. The answers to the questions will reveal your own personality and what partner is most likely for you. Please, do remember that compatibility between people has many factors, and if you have had a dynamic relationship with a sign that is not listed as one of your top three, then your charts should be examined more closely to see where the connections are. Enjoy the quiz.

1. **What qualities are most important to you in a sexual partner?**
   a Spontaneity and unpredictability
   b Sensuousness
   c Witty conversation
   d Expressiveness

2. **Sexually, which sense is most important to you for getting in the mood?**

   a The sight of an attractive face or body
   b The scent of cologne/perfume or a partner's skin
   c The sound of a sexy voice or listening to music
   d The way a partner touches you

3. **How do you approach your daily to-do list?**

   a I multitask—I never do just one thing at a time
   b I usually finish each project in a methodical, thorough manner and then move on to the next one
   c I work on something until I become bored with it, then I find something else to do
   d I get things done when I feel like it

4. **Which of the following describes what occurs when you lose your temper?**

   a I feel a short, intense burst of anger that goes away as quickly as it appears
   b I don't get angry often, but when I do, I explode
   c I internalize anger and feel anxious
   d I quietly suffer and usually end up crying

5. **Who would you most likely consider for a one-night stand?**

   a A sexy stranger you meet while traveling
   b Someone who reminds you of an old partner

c A close friend
d An old flame

6. **What one word best describes your sexual rhythm?**

    a Quick
    b Slow
    c Erratic
    d Waves

7. **When faced with a big decision, how do you handle it?**

    a I go with what my gut instincts tell me
    b I weigh all the pros and cons carefully
    c I ask everyone I know for an opinion
    d I feel it out and wait until the right decision reveals itself

8. **Where did your favorite childhood memories take place?**

    a Sports or cultural events
    b Outside
    c Social gatherings
    d Home

9. **Would you enjoy sex in a place where you might get caught?**

    a Yes
    b No

10. **What is your favorite way to spend a Sunday afternoon?**

   a Take a hike, go for a run, or play sports
   b Go out for brunch
   c Talk on the phone
   d Lie on the couch and watch movies

11. **If asked to perform or speak in front of people, how do you react?**

   a I glow with pleasure and confidence on stage
   b I do a competent job
   c I get stage fright but manage through the performance
   d I freeze with fear

12. **If someone looked in your closet, what would they find?**

   a An eclectic collection of costumes and everyday clothes
   b Neatly hung outfits
   c Clothes hung according to season/color
   d Old clothes that have sentimental value

13. **What do you think is your best physical feature?**

   a Long legs
   b Bottom
   c Neck and shoulders
   d Large breasts or pecs

14. **What physical feature interests you the most?**

    a Firm body
    b A well-defined behind
    c Sensuous lips
    d Defined shoulders and arms

15. **If you have a complaint, what is your most usual phrase?**

    a "It's not fair"
    b "I don't have enough"
    c "Things are boring"
    d "I don't feel well"

16. **What is the best lighting to put you in the mood?**

    a Daylight
    b Candlelight
    c Lighting doesn't matter
    d Total darkness

17. **What personality trait is most attractive to you in a mate?**

    a Generosity
    b Steadiness
    c Humor
    d Loyalty

18. **What would you consider adding to a relationship to spice things up?**

    a Fantasy role-play
    b A vibrator or sex toy
    c Pornography
    d None of the listed options

19. **Select one of the following words to complete this sentence: If life isn't _____, it's not worth it.**

    a Fast-paced
    b Secure
    c Funny
    d Emotional

20. **Which of the following sexual practices would you enjoy the least?**

    a Quick sex
    b Rough sex
    c Phone sex
    d Oral sex

21. **If you were hoping for a long-term relationship with someone, when would you most likely sleep together for the first time?**

    a On the first date
    b At the two-month mark
    c After three dates
    d Depends on my mood

22. **What do you consider an important prelude to good sex?**

   a Good jokes/laughing
   b A massage
   c Sexy talk
   d Dinner

23. **When is your favorite time to make love?**

   a Early in the morning
   b In the afternoon
   c In the evening, before going to sleep
   d In the middle of the night

24. **What best describes your general attitude toward life?**

   a Exuberant
   b Practical
   c Changeable
   d Sentimental

25. **Who are you most likely to be in your sexual fantasies?**

   a The hunter
   b The prostitute
   c Part of a ménage à trois
   d A damsel/bachelor in distress

26. **What do you wear to sleep after making love?**

   a Nothing
   b A nightie or pajamas

c Something belonging to your partner

d An old T-shirt

27. What do you consider a sexy scent?

a Citrus

b Vanilla

c Mint

d Patchouli

28. Would you ever consider adding a third partner?

a Yes

b No

29. How does the full moon make you feel?

a Passionate

b Sleepy

c Wildly alert

d Emotional

30. What is the strongest aphrodisiac for you?

a A sense of adventure

b Money

c Good looks

d Status

31. What kind of humor do you most enjoy?

a Practical jokes

b Slapstick

c Witty language

d Gallows humor

32. What's your favorite sexual position?

    a Partner on top
    b Doggie style
    c Everything
    d Missionary position

33. If you had to choose *one* word to describe your-self, what would it be?

    a Emotional
    b Mysterious
    c Courageous
    d Diplomatic
    e Impetuous
    f Humorous
    g Practical
    h Dedicated
    i Unique
    j Knowledgeable
    k Discerning
    l Intuitive

34. Which of the following turns you on the most?

    a Nibbling
    b Rubbing
    c Kissing
    d Tickling

35. **What is the most important part of a relationship between the sheets?**

   a The anticipation
   b The cuddling afterward
   c The pillow talk afterward
   d The orgasms

SCORING
a = 1 point   b = 2 points   c = 3 points   d = 4 points

Question 33:

Emotional = 2	Practical = 4
Mysterious = 2	Dedicated = 4
Courageous = 3	Unique = 1
Diplomatic = 1	Knowledgeable = 1
Impetuous = 3	Discerning = 4
Humorous = 3	Intuitive = 2

Add up your points for all thirty-five questions and find your most compatible signs in the following table.

Most Compatible Signs

Score	Most Compatible Signs	Other Interesting Possibilities
35–50	Gemini, Libra, Aquarius	Aries, Leo, Sagittarius
51–70	Cancer, Scorpio, Pisces	Taurus, Virgo, Capricorn
71–100	Aries, Leo, Sagittarius	Gemini, Libra, Aquarius
101–136	Taurus, Virgo, Capricorn	Cancer, Scorpio, Pisces

Now that you have a good idea about your preferences and the signs that you feel most attracted to, you can read this book with discernment. Check out your most compatible signs for insight into their preferences. Take a look at past sexual relationships and see if those relationships might have benefited from some astrological tips. And most of all, enjoy the myriad ways people express their passion and affection.

Chapter 1

Aries
(March 21–April 19)

Aries is numero uno and likes it that way. This is the first sign of the zodiac, and it begins at the vernal equinox. Aries's element is fire, and he blazes his trail with dashing verve. In ancient Greece, Ares was the name for the planet Mars and symbolized the god of war. Aries may appear to have calmed some bellicose tendencies, but in the bedroom, his warlike ancestors definitely predominate. The curled horns that grace the Ram are symbols of fertility and libido. Impetuosity is Aries's trademark.

The Conqueror

Aries is a leader and will be in hot pursuit of anyone who has caught his attention. Life and sex are contests to Aries, and it doesn't matter if the prize is just a kiss—he wants to win. All the fire signs are intuitive and inspirational in all areas of their lives. Aries is the first fire sign and leads the pack in terms of ardor and high energy.

From reveille in the morning, Aries is ready to charge through the day, investigating what potential partners she can charm and seduce into playing on her team. Aries wants her fiery energy to burn with someone, and like a frisky ram, she hunts for a partner to play with. She likes to conquer but not dominate. It is a fine distinction. She is not aggressive, but instead is extremely passionate, and welcomes someone who will seduce her after first showing a lack of interest. If her potential mate's lack of interest really is rejection, she will speedily leave for a more likely prospect, but until she gets that message, she will charge into the fray.

Written in the Stars

Aries loves spicy tastes. Seduction by chili pepper may not be listed in a sex manual, but try cooking or eating Mexican food consistently with your Aries. Chances are, you will have a great time in bed.

Aries is not an out-of-control sign and does not usually explode with temper the way Taurus can, but playful biting, slapping, wrestling, and fooling around with belts can be very alluring and sexy activities for Aries. He likes the pursuit of sex almost as much as the deed itself. With all his fire, he needs a lot of passionate contact; a cute cuddle or tame affection will not satisfy the Ram.

Moving from a one-night stand to a more consistent relationship is a challenge for Aries. It does happen, and if you are unsure what your status is, ask. Aries will be clear on this point, but can be persuaded to keep the fire going if there is enough spice between you.

What Turns Aries On—and Off

There is a certain sparkle in a person's eye when contemplating a fine time in bed. It can happen walking down the street when you catch someone's eye, or in the midst of a boring meeting, when that curly-haired cutie looks at you from across the conference table. This sparkle is a major turn-on for Aries. It promises everything and demands nothing. Getting together with Aries is easy because she is so turned on by the possibilities of sex with different people. She is a person of her word, so if she decides to be in a faithful, committed relationship, you can believe her, but until that time, playing the field is a delight.

Another turn-on is a quick-paced person. Aries does not like to hang around for languid or slow-moving people. He speaks quickly; expresses himself with large gestures; and likes to pop into bed, pop out, and then maybe pop in again. Getting bored is almost as painful for Aries as it is for Gemini. Aries can be a champagne partner: bubble, bubble, and then go flat. If Aries's interest and ardor wane, or his attention moves to something else, there is usually no getting things back on track. There are too many other people and possibilities waiting to be conquered.

Another turn-on is a physically fit body that can accommodate athletic and vigorous sex. You know those people who give you a firm handshake that is almost too firm, but it feels good? Aries in bed is like that—very definite energy and very definite wants. A major turn-on is deciding on the sexual plan of action and executing it. With Aries, there won't be much conversation, just a few agreed-upon cues, and full throttle ahead.

Written in the Stars

Aries are hot-blooded and can have higher-than-normal fevers when ill. This is the normal way their bodies repel infection. It also means that even when they are sick they are usually horny.

A turnoff for Aries is anyone who is a generic sex machine. A person who gets physical just to do it, without any consideration of the person and the fun leading up to it, will not appeal to Aries. Aries likes sex, but if it is without at least a feeling of camaraderie, the experience will not be satisfying or fun. A machine is cold, and Aries is hot.

Sexual role-playing is also a turnoff for Aries. She wants the real body-to-body experience without a lot of artifice. Besides, time spent putting the imagination to work to cook up a fantasy of the virgin and Attila the Hun could be better spent just enjoying each other between the sheets.

Aries is turned off by injustice. This consideration may not be evident for a romp in bed, but a person who may be attractive and sexy but treats other people in a snobbish or superior way will not find their way into Aries's heart or bed.

Aries's Strengths and Specialties

Sheer physical stamina is a great strength of Aries. Midnight, two p.m., six a.m., or afternoon delight—it is all hunky-dory with Aries. Aries also does not need much lead time. The time from the first tingle to getting into bed is usually quick and without complications. If Aries wants you and you are willing, there will not be a lot of coy foreplay or wooing. Think of Petruchio and Kate in Shakespeare's *The Taming of the Shrew*. He conquers, and she allows herself to be conquered. And in their fashion, they live happily ever after. Perhaps they were both Aries.

Oral pleasure is A-OK with Aries because it is a quick solution when there might not be enough time for the whole enchilada. Aries is wholeheartedly in favor of nipping into a handy closet for a quickie if the situation presents itself. She is not modest and is usually so charming that you won't be able to tell whether the flush on her face is from the great idea she has had or from a tryst in the supply closet.

Written in the Stars

In addition to peppery tastes, the smell of strong coffee and the spice cardamom are scents that Aries loves. Brew up a pot of coffee, and your Aries will make haste to get to you and the java.

Aries's Weaknesses and Foibles

As you may guess, Aries's love of speedy conclusions can be a weakness. An Aries guy may be so eager that he has a tendency to ejaculate prematurely. There is always another chance, and perhaps even another, but until you get the timing coordinated, this may be a problem. For those signs that love consistency and dependability, whether in the act or in a relationship, Aries is not the one for you. An Aries has too much energy to limit himself to one relationship until he decides to marry. When Aries is with a person he will give his all, but there may be a few others who are also receiving his all.

Aries is not keen on the finer points of lovemaking. Sensuality doesn't interest her as much as immediate hot and sudden sex, because her sexuality is hot and sudden. Stimulation can be from bodies, external sounds, and rhythms such as music or just percussion beats. Island sounds like a steel drum are especially evocative.

For Aries, sexual communication has to happen in the context of activity. Aries doesn't like to chat or have lengthy discussions about what worked and what didn't. He is helpless without the enthusiasm of doing. Talking is a mental activity and, therefore, boring. To work things out between you, try this approach. Take his hand, put it where you need it, and let nature takes its course. Aries will assume if you have long discussions that you just don't like him, and he will shut down the heater and scoot.

The Aries Man

Aries is by definition a masculine sign. The Aries guy is comfortable with being male and loves the fact that he is a boy. He will retain a boyish charm throughout his life. You will always know where you stand with an Aries fling, and everything up until marriage is a fling. There can be a brash quality to a lot of Aries men that belies the sensitivity beneath the Ram's energy. Aries men are not sentimentally sensitive, but they look out for the underdog and are protective. If an Aries sees someone he has the hots for and that person is being unfairly treated, it will add fuel to the pursuit. Saving a person, even if it leads to a fistfight, is a great turn-on for Aries.

> **Passion Points**
> Aries's head is an erogenous zone! Stroking the brow, luxuriating in the hair, kissing the nose, and massaging the ears and cheeks are special turn-ons.

In terms of style, Aries men like clothes that feel comfortable. He has a touch of the dashing and may enjoy clothes that are snazzy and suggestive of different historical time periods. Even if he is not very athletic, he will have sporty clothes.

Temper flare-ups are common with Aries men. They are not people who are full of rage, but instead they feel anger whenever the team lets them down, the world is unjust, and they don't get the partner they want. They get their problem off their chests and move on to the next campaign.

Lastly, Aries the conqueror wants to know that his battle equipment is grade A, in fine working order, and better than the other guy's. Compliments about this part of his anatomy are essential, not exactly because he feels insecure, but because it is a potent turn-on to know that, in your eyes, he ranks in the size and desirability department.

The Aries Woman

This woman was born a leader, even if she tries to be one of the gang. As mentioned previously, Aries is a masculine sign, and all that assertive energy in a woman cannot be corralled into being a nice, sweet girl. Before feminism, Aries women must have felt very frustrated. Now that there are many possibilities for expressing different sides of a woman's personality and sexuality, Aries women do not have to hide their drive for power and sexiness behind bouquets of violets or demure expressions.

These women have strong libidos and do not want to fool around waiting to be pursued. They can make the first move and will be thrilled when it is accepted, and courageous enough to keep going if it is rejected. They tend to be sports oriented and very active. If, for some inscrutable reason, your Aries Ram is shy, you may find that, in bed, her wild nature is liberated. It would be worth the effort to pursue this seemingly timid Aries.

Aries has a good sense of style, but nothing fussy or frilly will suit her. The Aries woman likes the tailored look, and loves simple, sexy black or red underwear.

She may love the idea of driving or riding a motorcycle with accompanying leather outfits. The Aries woman is all about a tough exterior and a sweet, powerfully sexy interior. She is not inhibited and is happy to have sex in unusual places. Sleeping naked after making love is usual. Fabric gets in the way of body-to-body cuddling.

On top or on the bottom, sideways, or oral pleasure—once the Aries woman gets going, her engines are strong, and she will turn to her partner with sheer delight in physical passion. She may say that she wants more than a one-night stand, but if there is not enough sexual energy between the two of you, she will move on without too many qualms. It simply is not fun for Aries to deal with a partner who can't match her ardor.

Beneath the tough exterior of an Aries woman is a child who can be hurt easily. The ego that is associated with Aries needs stroking, and she especially needs compliments and assurances that her sometimes tomboy sexuality is the best for you. She also wants to know that her breasts are just the right size for your hands.

Written in the Stars

Even in the foreplay department, Aries women may require less than women of other signs. She likes to get right to the point and can be bold about telling you what she wants.

Setting the Scene

There is no best place or scene for sex for Aries because the important thing is the act itself, and it can happen anywhere. An Aries can be in the midst of a team meeting or a party, or mowing the lawn, or playing sports. Suddenly a notion occurs to him, and he is on the phone or popping round to your place. He may not need to say much. He may have noticed a screened-in porch behind the bushes that conveniently has an air mattress on the floor. "Come on," he says, and you follow, wondering and hoping. Or maybe your Aries is a firefighter, and one day you visit the firehouse and he shows you an antique fire truck that happens to have a large back seat. All that leather! These unique places turn Aries on and are good for a change if the bedroom has gotten routine. Once you are both fired up, passion takes over, and there is not too much thinking or planning. Plunge ahead. If you challenge Aries to wear thigh-high boots, then she will do it. If you ask him to beat bongo drums with one hand and pleasure you with the other, he will enjoy the challenge. The major factor in setting the scene is desire; everything else is unimportant.

Sexy Matches: The Hot and Not-So-Hot Combinations

You will know right away if this is a hot or not-so-hot combo for you. Aries does not hide feelings or pretend out of politeness. If you feel this fling is not so hot, give it a try for a while, but if there is no fire, patience will not make it happen. No matter what anyone else says, if you and your partner have a spark, you will know it and enjoy it.

Aries and Aries

A bonfire of passion! These two fire signs are good matches and make energetic partners. They can keep up with each other and understand impetuous desires. The only drawback is that you will have to agree to alternate being the leader. If one time you are dominant, and the next it is the other Aries, then each of your me-first inclinations are honored. Also, two Aries together may butt heads over the smallest things, and it is difficult for either to give in. But settling these differences can be wild fun.

Aries and Taurus

Traditionally, fire and earth is not an easy combination, but Aries lights up and amuses Taurus. This combo can be hot because Taurus likes the spark Aries offers. It is good for a fling or a one-night stand as, over time, Aries's fast pace will weary Taurus. Aries will also stretch Taurus's sexual repertoire to the limit. Both signs are physically strong and have good libidos. For a time, they can enjoy their differences. It may not last, but it will be a good love affair.

Aries and Gemini

Fire and air combined with a leadership—cardinal—sign (Aries) and a changeable—mutable—sign (Gemini) mean infinite sexual variety. The combination of these signs might exhaust anyone else because they spin off each other so well. Aries will be glad to lead Gemini into a hot relationship, and Gemini will happily follow.

Both signs are fearless sexual experimenters and believe in physical fun. The signs match each other in playfulness, but Aries is the more passionate sign. Unfortunately, flighty Gemini can fool Aries into thinking there is love when Gemini is playing the trickster.

Aries and Cancer

Fire (Aries) can make water (Cancer) boil, but water can also put out the fire. This is a not-so-hot combination because the sexual energy of each sign requires very different stimuli. Aries is of the moment, and Cancer wants a steady stream of past history to feel comfortable enough to be intimate. For sex based on aggressive tension, this combination works for a while, but the two signs don't really harmonize. Aries thinks Cancer is too much work, and Cancer thinks Aries is too insensitive.

When Stars Align

If you have gotten to first base with an Aries man, keep the sense of pursuit going. The chase is always part of the sexual merry-go-round that the Aries man enjoys.

Aries and Leo

A happy trine or pairing of red and yellow fire, Aries and Leo complement each other because they are of the same element. There is an inherent competition with these two signs. Aries says, "Me first," Leo says, "Look at me," and unless they really work hard, the competition extends into bed. Someone has to give in. Usually it will be Leo, because she will feel it is the magnanimous thing to do. This combo is good for short, hot affairs, and once everything is cooking, a long-term relationship could easily follow.

Aries and Virgo

This is an irritating combination that leaves neither sign satisfied. The elements are fire and earth, but the culprit that makes Aries and Virgo not so hot is their very different needs. Virgo needs careful detailed planning, and Aries hates anything that smacks of schedules and routine. A late-night affair at the office might be an exciting experience, but more than that will frustrate both signs. Virgo will get off on trying to organize Aries, and Aries will delight in upsetting Virgo's carefully laid plans. This is a search-and-destroy mission, rather than a coming together.

Aries and Libra

The opposites of fire and air here definitely attract each other. This is a sexy affair and a relationship with growth potential if both partners want to mature. It is not a given that Aries and Libra will take up the challenge. Aries says, "Me," and Libra says, "We." You can understand the dichotomy between the two positions. Although each fans the other's flames, there is conflict. But their planetary rulers, Mars and Venus, are the archetypical male and female planets, and that makes for good sex and lots of creative sparks. Aries and Libra could spend a long time battling this one out, with a lot of good times in the sack in the meantime.

Aries and Scorpio

This is a hot, hot—maybe too hot—combo. Even though their elements of fire and water are different, Aries and Scorpio can go where most people don't dare to go. They can be fearless sexual warriors, and neither will shrink from a challenge sexually. If Aries wants whips, Scorpio says, "Let's try chains." If Scorpio says, "Let's do it in the shower," Aries says, "Why not the pool?" The one-upmanship between these signs means lots of creative and possibly kinky sex. Not every Aries and Scorpio is a sexual titan, but the explosive potential exists. These signs like to explore dominance and submission. After a time, a relationship between these signs usually doesn't have legs because it is too yang.

> **Written in the Stars**
> A particularly enjoyable scent for Aries women is the peppery scent of geranium. That and the smell of fresh ginger will get all her juices flowing.

Aries and Sagittarius

These two signs make good-natured partners. They both are fire signs, and each helps the other feel expansive. They meet with their considerable enthusiasm for life and lust and are happy to play together. Aries may be the leader, but Sagittarius rarely feels dominated. If

Sagittarius doesn't like something, he just gets on his horse and goes. Aries respects Sagittarius's policy of zero tolerance to compromises in life, likes Sagittarius's built-in BS meter, and wants to behave exactly the same. Both signs like motion and the opportunity to be sexual in different environments. They don't take life too seriously, and that translates into good bedroom fun. Long term, their great asset is that each knows how to prevent boredom.

Aries and Capricorn

This combo is lusty but difficult. If you narrow your focus to just what happens between the sheets, Aries and Capricorn can have a very good time. They are leadership signs with very different planetary rulers: Mars and Saturn. But think about the ram and the goat; each is a lusty animal. The area of conflict is rhythm and decorum. Aries does not like to spend long sessions exploring another's anatomy. He goes for the gold and then moves on. And Aries does not care who knows or sees his sexual inclinations toward the Goat. He is impetuous and wants to flaunt his flame. Capricorn shudders at this lack of decorum. Saturn wants to fit in with the world, and Aries is interested in leading the world. Keep this love affair a secret if you can, and it will be hot for a while.

Aries and Aquarius

Fire and air are usually hot together, and it is true that these two signs can excite each other. This is not one of the all-time hot combos, because Aries is so personally oriented, and Aquarius so group oriented. Aries does not get the detached coolness of Aquarius and may spend fruitless nights trying to arouse him to the ardor that is the life's breath for Aries. It doesn't work. Between these two signs, passion can be momentarily hot because they both understand erratic impulses, and the lack of consistency between the two is a turn-on. At the end of the night, the creative spark is not hot enough to make a good combination for long.

Aries and Pisces

The next-door-neighbor signs are in different elements: fire and water. They can work together because Aries compensates for Pisces's lack of vigor. Aries likes leading Pisces into the nitty-gritty of physical passion. Pisces has her own way of being sexual, but it is not hot and sweaty like Aries. The two can tease and tickle each other, and it will work because they come from different planets. However, in the long run it's a no-go between the Fish and the Ram. One is on land, and the other in the sea.

Sex Planets: Mars and Venus

To get the full scoop on sexual chemistry, find out where Mars and Venus are for you and your partner. Considering this as well as the Sun sign will increase your understanding of a partner's and your own libido.

Mars in Aries

Mars is the ruler in Aries. The energy flows red-hot and is very assertive. This sign placement must be physical, either with sports or with bedroom Olympics. There are usually great shows of passion and directed pursuit toward the object of his affection and desire. Consistency is not typical. Mars in Aries cannot bear to be frustrated and has no patience in dealing with long, laborious negotiations either for business or sex. "Let's get going" is his favorite phrase, and he can be so fired up that he doesn't notice that he's stepping on someone's toes. When he does realize there's an issue, he will apologize profusely but not slow down. Sexually speaking, Mars in Aries will love hot, quick sex in a variety of settings. If the notion strikes him in the midst of a ball game, for example, he will start looking for a convenient nook or cranny. Why wait, he says to himself, and if you feel daring, it will be a hot encounter. If you are not interested, he will pursue you at first, but he won't persist if he's definitely rejected.

Written in the Stars

Mars in Aries loves caps and hats. Give them as gifts, and play sexy games with different hats. Commemorate occasions in your romance with a monogrammed baseball cap. Favorite colors, of course, lean toward the reds.

Mars in Aries may be prone to rash decisions and is very temperamental. He has a bad habit of picking fights for the pleasure of asserting his power. He may never duke it out with someone but will argue a point on principle until he feels he has won. If this talent is on the side of truth and justice, it is a formidable foe. But if it is in search of getting a hot, fresh cup of coffee, it is terribly misplaced.

Venus in Aries

This planetary position sparkles with fireworks and sex appeal. There is a rugged strength to people with this position. Aries men and women are pals as well as partners, and are usually very athletic. They can be good tap dancers! If you want her to tap dance all over your body, the lure of adventure and fun is a powerful aphrodisiac. She will almost swagger when she walks and will have very few inhibitions about expressing desire. Alas, as with all Aries placement, consistency is not her strong point. Unless she is constantly stimulated sexually, mentally, and emotionally, she is a hard one to keep burning for you. If this is a turn-on for you, expect lots of late-night romps and impromptu afternoon adventures.

A woman with this placement may find that the outside world may need some time to get used to her assertive manner. She may grow up feeling she doesn't fit in because she doesn't feel very girly. An occupation that allows her to express herself physically will help in this regard. Finding a partner who can match her energy will not be difficult. The difficulty is keeping her interested. Venus in Aries's sign is not an easy fit, but it certainly can be exciting.

Chapter 2

Taurus
(April 20–May 20)

Taurus, the second sign of the zodiac, is one of the powerhouse signs in astrology and in sexual activity. As a fixed sign, Taurus may not be flashy, but he is very definite, rooted in his senses and what feels pleasurable. Taurus demonstrates his fixity with his will and drive. Material comfort and well-being are essential for Taurus. He won't feel sexy or willing unless there is money in the bank, food in the refrigerator, and a secure job or prospects for the future.

The Sensualist

In ancient times, the bull was a fertility symbol and was worshipped for his power and sexiness. Ancient pottery depicts athletic games including bull wrestling and leaping over and under a bull. There are many myths about the sexually potent bull. The rumor that Taurus is stubborn is true, but to the Bull's mind, stubbornness is just good sense: why change unless you have to?

> **Written in the Stars**
>
> Pheromones are nature's way for partners to attract each other. Some scientists have posited that using heavy deodorants and scented soaps challenges the natural scents that bring people together for sex.

Taurus is an earth sign and, of all the signs, the most connected to the sense of touch. Taurus will walk into a clothes shop and immediately touch all the different fabrics. In her own home or yours, she enjoys caressing the pillows, the sofa covers, or the wood, or even gliding her hand over marble or granite counters to enjoy their cool feel. She also enjoys casually touching people in the course of a conversation. As you might guess, the single greatest turn-on for Taurus is how a person feels. She wants to touch and caress skin, hair, chest, and bottom, and it will all be equally pleasurable. Also, being touched all over is a major turn-on.

A Taurus is also highly influenced by a sense of smell. If you recall the sign's symbol, the Bull, you can imagine him putting his head in the air and catching the scent of a cow, a matador, or a delicious patch of grass. Translated into bedroom terms, a special perfume or cologne is a strong turn-on. Taurus has a strong libido, so just a whiff will do. Another Taurus turn-on is the body's natural smell. Good old sweat from working in a garden or at the gym is an aphrodisiac.

What Turns Taurus On—and Off

Taurus's planetary ruler, Venus, also rules all manner of luxury, as well as how a person socializes. Everyone's chart has the planet Venus, but not everyone has her in an easy sign. It is a turn-on for Taurus to be in comfortable surroundings, with good food, soft music, convivial company, and dim lights. After the guests leave, it is time for Taurus and partner to waltz into the bedroom. The memory of the food, wine, and socializing adds luster to the lovemaking that follows. Fill each of Taurus's senses, and you have a contented, turned-on man or woman.

Taurus is turned on by money. Not necessarily greedy, she is conscious of good value. Make-believe scenarios like buying sexual favors at a price gets both partners' imaginations going. Negotiating the deals for what buys which favor could take all night, and is a lusty turn-on.

Turnoffs for Taurus are leathery skin or a partner who doesn't care for their skin. Also, a person who always wears itchy wool or synthetic fabric will not invite the best feeling in Taurus. Taurus is a security-minded sign and wants to know the parameters of the game before plunging ahead. Just sex is fine, but if she feels that the partner is manipulating her for security or material gain, it will be a total turnoff in the bedroom.

> **Written in the Stars**
> Wearing sweet scents that are associated with tastes like vanilla is a double turn-on for Taurus.

Taurus is also turned off by someone being prissy or putting on airs. The Bull likes a natural feel to all relationships and is not impressed by manners. Being polite superficially betokens an insensitive nature to Taurus. Any kind of artificial behavior gives Taurus the sense that sex will be efficient and tidy, and that is a Taurus turnoff. This is a sign that does not like to feel monitored. Too many instructions or requests gets the Bull's stubbornness going and shuts down his natural warmth and sexiness. Additionally, if something requires too much effort to learn or seems strained, Taurus will be turned off. Sex toys and paraphernalia, even though they might be pleasurable, are not as interesting to Taurus as being with a person skin to skin, with all senses open.

Taurus's Strengths and Specialties

First off, Taurus has incredible body strength and will be happy to use it in the pursuit of pleasure. This is a sign that loves to languish and spend lazy time with a partner. Making love comes naturally with Taurus's soft, sensual feelings. Taurus also has a reputation as a wonderful cook, and his sense of taste is as developed as the sense of touch. Eating of all kinds is a specialty. If you want to please a Taurus, consider buying a chocolate fountain from which you can spoon warm chocolate and drizzle it everywhere.

The ears are particularly sensitive and always a good place to begin. Taurus could be happy for quite a while with kisses and nuzzling all around the ears and neck. And as a lovemaking rhythm gets more and more intense, Taurus may enjoy rubbing his ears against his partner's neck or cheek.

Taurus's Weaknesses and Foibles

Once things get started, Taurus may charge ahead and not be very interested in who finishes first and who has to play catchup. As far as Taurus is concerned, there will be other times to get the timing exact, and she doesn't want to spoil the mood with discussion or recriminations for what might work perfectly well the next time around.

This is a romantic sign that will retreat quickly if she doesn't feel that her efforts were well received. Taurus is interested in a partner's pleasure but doesn't want to think about mechanics or anything that didn't go well. Solo touching and soft caresses are good enough until next time if one or the other's timing is off. Taurus is the original don't-make-a-big-deal-of-things sign.

Passion Points
The outside of the ear holds pressure points that relate to the entire spinal column. Caress and rub the ear, starting from the earlobe, and the entire body relaxes.

The Taurus Man

This man is a solid citizen who is romantic, sensual, and interested in sex as a prelude to a relationship. He might play the field in his twenties, but by the time he turns thirty, he wants the comfort of a home, a partner, work, and regular sex. His nature is cuddly, and you will notice that the Taurus man frequently touches people casually. More intimate contact will be filled with hugs, kisses, massage, and good naked sex. If you spend the night, don't bother with nightwear, as Taurus wants to feel skin for as much time as you have together.

Physically, Taurus is strong and likes athletic love-making. Oral sex is always an appetizer, and if there isn't much time, it will have to do. The Taurus man enjoys longer bouts of lovemaking, but better a little sucking than nothing! He is also a casual person, and a partner wearing a soft flannel shirt and worn jeans is fine with him. He may prefer a natural look, and a little mud or dirt can be sensually exciting. When Taurus's sensuality heats up, he may get into doggy-style sex. He likes the full expression of sexual positions. He also can be a vocal partner with appreciative moans, murmurs, and shouts.

> ### Written in the Stars
> Taurus is normally a placid, calm sign, but when Taurus loses his temper, no one wants to be around the explosion. It may happen only a few times in a lifetime, but when it does, clear out and wait for it to pass. Sex is not usually the reason a Taurus gets angry, and if he is in a temper, do not try to kiss and make it better. He will have to cool down on his own time and usually will, for Taureans do not stay angry for long.

The Taurus Woman

Taurus women love physical sensation, both giving and receiving. You will recognize these women by their sustained energy and love of the outdoors. This is one sign that would not mind at all sneaking into a private garden shed and making love. Being with nature and doing what comes naturally is a double pleasure.

The Taurus woman is very interested in finding what pleases her partner and will remember anything her partner mentions to her. She usually loves to cook and feels a good dinner is the best prelude to a sexy night. Silky lingerie in pale blue or yellow will excite a Taurus woman and make her feel especially alluring.

> **Written in the Stars**
> In the nineteenth century, private dining rooms sported doors that closed without door handles. After dinner, it was expected that the lord and lady would stay and make love and not want to be disturbed. Sounds like a Taurean woman thought this up!

Setting the Scene

Imagine a parlor decorated in the style of *The Arabian Nights* with low divans covered in soft, blue fabric and an arching canopy of gauzy, yellow material creating a tent effect over the whole room. The shelves are full of beautiful books, childhood mementos, vinyl records, pottery, and vases. There is very little space in the room that is not filled. The lamps have stained glass shades that cast pools of soft light. Bowls of fruit, nuts, M&M's, or granola mix are always handy. You and your partner walk into this cozy paradise, turn on a soft pink light, put on some samba music, and then, with one whiff of scent, you are both in the mood. Touching begins with kisses on the throat and neck. Continuing with a samba striptease, you are both naked and skin to skin. You quickly move to the divan, and there you both stay. Maybe there is a pause and you order takeout. One appetite leads to the next, and all of a sudden, it is the middle of the night. Why bother to go home? You fall asleep and dream of green fields and contented cows.

Sexy Matches: The Hot and Not-So-Hot Combinations

If you are unhappy about one of the not-so-hot combos listed here, keep in mind you may defy the odds. Trust yourself and see where life takes you.

Taurus and Aries

These two signs go about life in very different ways, but the combination of the two can be exciting. Aries fuels Taurus's fires because of his endearing charm and enthusiasm.

Passion Points
Erogenous zones are the hair and forehead. Aries loves to have his whole head and face caressed. And Taurus, as you know, goes nuts for the ears and throat.

When Aries suggests that they duck into a convenient closet for a quickie, somehow Taurus's reticence disappears because Aries is so naively appealing. This situation is stimulating for Taurus and confirms to Aries that he has the pizzazz he always knew he had. Let's call this a shipboard affair: it lasts for a time and then remains as a fabulous memory.

Taurus and Taurus

Good, passionate, trustworthy, dependable, and utterly comfortable. This is an easy combination for all sorts of connections. Because both people are attuned to their senses, they mirror each other's desire without a lot of unnecessary preliminaries. Two Tauruses are like soft flannel shirts; they get better with age. If you both get into a rut or feel bored, try wearing edible underwear—and make it a surprise which one of you wears it.

Taurus and Gemini

Taurus and Gemini are fun together, but are not cut from the same cloth. Their elements, earth and air, do not sync up. The mental delight Gemini takes in learning about everything strikes Taurus as busywork that does not leave enough time for sensual play and love. This combo is fine for a one-night thrill but usually lacks staying power. The one point where Gemini and Taurus meet would be all connections with the mouth. Both signs are oral—kissing, sucking, or nipping all over the body is a satisfying way to explore and feel pleasure for both signs.

Taurus and Cancer

These two signs, ruled by Venus and the Moon, respectively, have a lot to give each other in sex and love. They share a slower rhythm and can feel lazy and sensual together. Cancer's sensitive tummy is a place Taurus loves to pay attention to, so both signs are content. Taurus and Cancer are hardwired for secure relationships, so this usually will not be a combination that leads only to a short-lived relationship. Also, there will not be much controversy over where to make love: it will be home or some other comfortable, secure spot. A motel or any place that feels transient will inhibit both partners. Both Cancer and Taurus need to be in familiar surroundings to unleash their sexual, affectionate natures. The Cancerian may prove to be too emotional and fluid for Taurus sometimes, but certainly the two signs can enjoy each other's giving natures.

Taurus and Leo

Both these signs are fixed, but in different elements. They usually do not go together well for relationships, but at an office party, when people have had too many beers, one glance could send these two people into a private room for unexpected sex. Taurus will be surprised. Leo will feel she has had contact with a sensual part of her nature that she didn't know about before, and the whole affair will pass away and remain a delightful memory. This is a quick contact, but while the relationship is happening, both signs like particular attention paid to the small of the back.

Taurus and Virgo

Earth to earth is a harmonious and easy connection.
Virgo, however, being ruled by Mercury, can be too
demanding and perfectionistic for laid-back Taurus.
Taurus does not react well to specific requests, such
as something listed in a sex manual. If Taurus can get
Virgo in the mood, then sex will be satisfying, and both
signs will share affection and good lovemaking. This
is not an overwhelmingly passionate combination,
because there is not as much aggression when these
signs get together as with other signs. Taurus and Virgo also both meet in the delights of good, healthy food.
Remember those dining rooms with no door handles!

Taurus and Libra

Although the elements of earth and air are usually
not an immediate turn-on, these signs share Venus as
their ruler and make a good duo. Not only will both
partners have good sexual chemistry, but they will also
have many tastes and activities in common. They share
a love of romance and enjoy candlelit dinners and long
walks on the beach or in the woods. Sex between Taurus
and Libra tends to be discreet. Neither of these signs is

interested in exhibitionism or anything extreme. Also, both Taurus and Libra want to have enough time when they get together. A date that is rushed and without preliminaries is not satisfying to either sign. The best turn-on for both signs is going out somewhere elegant and then retiring to the bedroom. As Libra and Taurus share so many other sensibilities, a Libra may be happy to have Taurus in the dominant position.

Passion Points

The neck and throat area is an especially sensitive one for Taurus. Taurus needs to cover her neck against the cold, but when she unwraps her scarf and exposes a vulnerable spot, she wants it kissed and caressed.

Taurus and Scorpio

This is a very frequent combination, as Taurus and Scorpio are opposite signs, and opposites attract. With these two powerhouse and willful signs, there is a lot of sexual chemistry. A Scorpio's intense desire finds a soothing partner in Taurus's lusty sensuality. Scorpio is a powerhouse sign also and will express sexuality with great strength and passion. Whatever fantasies are in the recesses of either person's mind can come to fruition with this combination. Scorpio might want to tie Taurus to a chair and play a love scene with all sorts of innuendos, and Taurus will go along with it because earthy instincts will always know when enough is enough. Scorpio is a hard sign to trust, but Taurus does because they both have formidable strength and can alternate who is the dominant partner.

Taurus and Sagittarius

This combination is not usually satisfying for either the long or short term. Taurus is a fixed sign, and Sagittarius is a mutable sign. The mutable signs are changeable and hard to pin down. This conflict, together with the lack of harmony in the elements, makes the Bull and the Archer less than compatible sexually. Sagittarius is too busy and too freedom loving to make Taurus feel comfortable. Also, Sagittarius likes a variety of settings and is easily bored with the regular and comfortable. With a Sagittarius, Taurus will have fun only if he is willing to be as flexible as he can manage.

> **When Stars Align**
> Remember that all earth signs love tactile stimulation. With Taurus, Virgo, and Capricorn, bring out the bear rug, mink coat, or faux-fur comforter.

Taurus and Capricorn

The earthy similarity between these two signs means that they naturally speak the same language and have an easy familiarity. There is good potential for lust here. Both will enjoy the natural smells of the other's body. The armpits are a turn-on. Taurus's cuddliness soothes the Capricorn tendency to bear the weight of the world on his shoulders. A back rub leading to kisses to the shoulders will get both the Bull and the Goat aroused. Tickling is another way to begin and will bring out the best in each sign.

Taurus and Aquarius

This combination is not so hot. Earth and air are the two elements, and although both signs are fixed, Aquarius is too mentally focused and eccentric for Taurus. Taurus also tends to be possessive, and Aquarius has lots of friends and needs to feel able to experiment with all of them, perhaps simultaneously. If these two do get together, Taurus will have to be the more flexible of the pair. Aquarius can be a law unto himself.

Taurus and Pisces

Venus and Neptune are the two planets ruling these respective signs. Theirs is a dreamy combination, with great sensuality and tender sex. Pisces loves anything that enhances the senses, such as wine, scents, and candles. Taurus also gravitates to sensual stimulants. Retreating to an underground lair with black sheets and a waterbed would be this couple's idea of heaven for a time. Pisces's big toe may be an unexpected erogenous zone. When sex is over, though, Taurus may, from time to time, be irritated by Pisces's dreamy and slippery character, but there is an opportunity between the two for short- and long-term relationships.

Sex Planets: Mars and Venus

To learn more about yourself and your partner, figure out in which sign his or her Venus and Mars are located. This information will add spicy tidbits to everything you have learned about your partner's Sun sign.

Mars in Taurus

When the planet of aggression, Mars, is placed in the sign of Taurus, a strong sex drive is present. The animal (that is, the bull) nature is very potent, and the usual finesse and soft and languid touch of Taurus is roughed up a bit. This is a placement that won't mind rolling in the hay or giving in to passion anywhere it might arise. If that happens to be outdoors in a field, that's where sex will take place. Mars in Taurus is not interested in polite dating routines. The sign's love of good food is also inextricably linked to feeling amorous. After a good steak and some wine, Mars in Taurus is ready to open all of his senses and share them with a partner.

Although Mars in Taurus is aggressive in pursuit, this is not a violent placement, but instead one interested in maximizing pleasure. Mars in Taurus doesn't need silky underwear or stimulating pictures to arouse desire. Full-body contact so that he or she can feel skin is the best way to satisfy Mars in Taurus. He will also be happy to use the same positions over and over. Mars in Taurus says: "If it feels good, why bother to change?" This is a sexy placement and needs a sexy partner.

Mars in Taurus likes the dominant position; positions that may be interesting but feel awkward aren't of interest.

Venus in Taurus

With Venus in Taurus, the sex drive is refined. These people have a strong libido, but, as Venus rules romance as well as the arts, sex is more sedate with this placement. Venus in Taurus requires more foreplay, a nice setting, soft fabrics, and all the trappings of seduction before getting into bed. She will also need a comfortable bed and soft music. Almond massage oil behind the ears is a great way to get things going.

This placement is not daring and won't want to fool around with any outrageous practices. It is a sensual placement and enjoys the comfort of holding, kissing, and lovemaking. The lips are very sensitive, and slow kisses, with attention to the eyes and ears, would feel dreamy.

Chapter 3

Gemini
(May 21–June 20)

The first air sign, Gemini is probably the most sexually playful sign of the zodiac. His planet, Mercury, delights in communication and loves confusing people. In ancient times, Mercury, or (in Greek) Hermes, was associated with a trickster personality. Today, we can see that the Gemini Twins love to play games, especially when they involve sex. Gemini's dual nature means that he can easily shift roles and enter into whatever sexual fantasies you or he might like to spin.

The Communicator

Communication for Gemini takes many forms. There are the funny voices she can turn on or off; there is talking about people, love, and sex; and there is thinking about sex, like wondering if people do it the same way in Borneo, or imagining a scenario when the pretty waitress or hunky trainer passes by. The daily life of a Gemini is filled with thoughts of possible seduction. Sometimes, a fling with Gemini consists entirely of a witty and engaging conversation. These mercurial people receive energy from the act of talking, and in certain cases, a stimulating conversation is almost as good as being physically intimate.

If you are in a long-term relationship with a Gemini, you might notice that social occasions where she can talk to many different types of people leave her brimming with energy as if she had had sex. Well, in a sense she has, because the energy of talking is a sexual experience for Gemini. If you are the recipient of a Gemini's infatuation, listen to her talk. Interrupting the flow of words will turn Gemini off, and she is not likely to want to get close to you at all.

Written in the Stars

Not strong physically, Gemini has to nourish his nervous system. If he is near a lot of smoke and air pollution, his system will suffer and he won't feel very sexy.

59

Gemini has a surprising personality and a very low boredom threshold. He must keep on the move physically, mentally, and sexually. He can be faithful in a committed relationship, but before he does such a thing, he wants to experience lots of flirting and lots of flings. The sign is masculine, but because of the dual (male and female) nature of the Twins, you may notice an androgynous quality in many Geminis. Fluid sexual tendencies may be present with many Gemini people, and they are happy to experiment.

When you and your Gemini are between the sheets, expect her to ask whether you like this or that, or if you have a better idea. She can be very bold in trying all types of sexual activity. Then she checks out the experience and determines whether it was interesting or not. Anything that was not interesting will not be repeated.

What Turns Gemini On—and Off

Singing, whispering, laughing, doing funny voices, whistling, ear blowing, imitating foreign accents, and expressing a clever turn of phrase are the foreplay choices for Gemini. Once his mind is engaged and you have communication between you, then energy can move away from the mouth and down the body to equally pleasurable areas. This will happen quickly if it is going to happen. Gemini does not belabor or delay anything. Of course, oral stimulation is a basic part of any sexual encounter for Gemini. The sense of touch is very light with Gemini, and a gentle caress on the breast or stroke of the cheek will be enough to start the motors humming. It is also a turn-on for Gemini to hear conversation from the street or in the next room as background atmosphere. Music or the sound of waves will keep him mentally engaged while he is making love. Gemini does not like silence.

Gemini can easily enter into role-playing fantasy, and it is a major turn-on. The key ingredient is a sense of play. Usually, intense bondage or discipline scenarios don't appeal to her, because Gemini isn't interested long enough in sensations that might hurt. However, if her partner is into it, no problem. Gemini is also turned on by a spontaneous "I didn't know we were going to do that" approach to sex. There will be no method to her pleasure, and if you catch her and are not flexible, be prepared for some adjustments.

> **Written in the Stars**
> Whether or not your climate is hot, having a ceiling fan on is always a soothing noise for Gemini. She also likes the feeling of moving air currents. Decorate your room with a mobile high overhead so that from many positions, Gemini can see shapes moving in the breeze.

A major turnoff is someone who speaks slowly or takes a long time to heat up sexually. When the notion comes to Gemini, he is ready and willing. He can do fun foreplay for a while, but once sex is in motion, it usually goes to a quick conclusion. There is a good possibility of an encore, but if his partner is always slower, that won't suit Gemini's sense of speed. Another turnoff will be any heavy conversations of what didn't go well. With Gemini, the way you speak about sex is as important as the sex itself. Try having pet names for favorite positions or body parts. That way you can say, "Well, the ring-a-ding-ding was pretty good, but let's try the king in his castle again." Speaking in this personal sex code will make Gemini pant for more. Gemini is also turned off by fussy plans or rigid schedules. Take advantage of the moment is his motto, and if you miss the moment, it's no action for you.

Gemini's Strengths and Specialties

In a word, a Gemini's strength is her tongue. She can use it in all the ways you can imagine, and then come up with a few you never thought of. The sign's love of oral sensation translates easily to sexual pleasure everywhere. Variety is the spice of life, and sex, for Gemini. She will not bore you and will expect the same in return. Different positions, different atmospheres, and different tastes all will keep your relationship exciting and fun. Gemini has a great ability to tease and tickle. Handholding, making dirty gestures, or even stimulating manually under the table at social functions if you are bored could be a romantic sport for Gemini. That way you both can keep your private sex world going and don't have to pay attention to uninteresting people.

The phone, text messaging, and email are all sex toys for Gemini. She loves to keep a steady stream of sexy dialogue going. That way, by the time you get together, all systems are on alert and primed for activity.

Gemini's Weaknesses and Foibles

Physically, Gemini usually tends toward leanness and doesn't feel quite solid. He moves so quickly that half the battle in making love is to catch him. Don't expect bear hugs or clingy behavior. Gemini moves into your life, connects, delivers his message of pleasure, and more than likely moves on. His energy is very charming but can be superficial. He is a master of sexual fantasy when his motor is revved up. The actual deed should happen quickly. In-depth feeling is not his strong suit. For water signs who may like silence after lovemaking, Gemini takes some getting used to. The relaxation of sex stimulates him to talk, even if he may not make a lot of sense.

The Gemini Man

As a partner, there are usually two major long-lasting partnerships in the Gemini man's life. Catch him in between these two, and you will have a very good time. The Gemini man has a powerful interest in information about everything. He gathers facts, trivia, and theories, and thrives on keeping up on the news and reading magazines. He may be thoroughly versed in a few subjects but will know a little about a whole lot more. Sex is a subject that interests him, and he will be proud of his knowledge and eager to put it into practice. These guys can be wild, especially if they get a hold of a sexy book or movie. Oral interests are strong. Their nervous structures are sensitive so they may be very speedy when first with a partner. But Gemini loves to do things in twos, so another opportunity will soon come your way.

Passion Points

A Gemini man will usually have long tapered and elegant hands. Touching them could be the start of a more in-depth relationship. He will also want to use his hands in unusual ways as part of the deluxe Gemini sex package.

The Gemini man loves to flirt and tease and will be outrageously imaginative in terms of the compliments he pays you. If you laugh at his jokes, you will be well on your way to a relationship. Gemini wants to feel mentally tantalized by a partner, and it is a wonderful game to try out any scenario that catches his fancy. A love affair will be fun, engaging, and brief.

The Gemini Woman

A Gemini woman can be very uninhibited and is not overly concerned who knows it. She loves to quip about sex, and she loves to put her quips into practice. Remember, Gemini is a masculine sign, and this is very evident in the Gemini woman's approach to sex. She enjoys pursuit, seduction, and flirting, but is happy to take an active part in the sexual dance. She does not tend to be demure and may find talking trashy a turn-on for herself and her partner. She can be a wanton tease. If you are interested in a female Gemini, make a move quickly, or you will be misled and then rejected.

Written in the Stars
It is a sometimes-unpleasant observation that Gemini equates insults with intimacy. If he gets on a verbal roll, he can be very hurtful. When you call him on it, he will say, "I was only joking." It is not intentional cruelty, but rather is an annoying habit. If you notice this trait, the only thing to do is toughen up, plug your ears, or go to another room.

Gemini women's style is simple, and they usually have very good figures and a little black dress that shows it off nicely. They like solid, muted colors as well as black and white. Pale blue usually suits their complexions. A Gemini woman can have two partners at the same time, but her preferred way to do this is to have each in a separate city. A little distance and motion keeps things manageable.

Setting the Scene

After a unique date such as a car rally or a lecture on building windmills, you and Gemini will be happy to go any place with a modicum of privacy. It could be your place, a hotel, a roadside inn, a deserted beach cabana, or a back corner of the library stacks. Wherever you end up, the space should have lots of windows and a ceiling fan. Daylight or a well-lit space is preferable because Gemini likes the turn-on of seeing her partner. As you walk to the site, the hand caress begins. Or perhaps you are meeting at a special place. Then, expect a steady stream of text messages, or chats on the cell, beforehand. By the time you get together, you are both ready, and you may not even make it to the bed. The living room floor is fine. The beach cabana with the sound of the waves is excellent; even a nearby kitchen counter will do the trick. When the moment comes, Gemini acts. You and your Gemini are laughing and speaking in all sorts of different voices. Then the comedy is interrupted by deepening pleasure as the mouth and tongue find other activities. Then there's a pause; then you continue. And so the night goes between jokes, laughter, and sex.

Sexy Matches: The Hot and Not-So-Hot Combinations

Gemini is generally a sexy sign because she is so experimental. There are better combinations than others, but if your combo isn't listed as hot, don't despair. A relationship with a Gemini is probably the most changeable of the zodiac. Read the following combinations to maximize pleasure and minimize strife.

Gemini and Aries

These two fan each other's flames as Gemini's element, air, feeds Aries's element, fire. There may be ferocious discussions about what turns them both on and whispered words about the best technique, but when it comes down to getting physical, these two signs like a quick date, and then another and another. Their rhythms are in sync. Gemini can't stand to be bored, and Aries can't stand to wait. Expect lots of oral pleasure and lots of jokes. Laughing and tickling might be all the preliminaries these two hot signs need.

Gemini and Taurus

The next-door-neighbor signs of Gemini and Taurus have different elements, air and earth. There is potential for good sexual chemistry here because Gemini amuses Taurus. For a fling or wild evening of unpredictable sex, this combo is okay. Taurus's solid nature, though, usually turns off Gemini's creativity and whimsy for anything longer than a one-night stand. The sexual ground where these two meet is the feel of skin. Gemini has very sensitive skin, and Taurus loves to touch it.

Gemini and Gemini

This is a polygamous relationship by definition because there are four partners: the two Geminis and their twins. Geminis immediately recognize their own, and there is a great sexual charge between them. They can talk, play games, amuse themselves, and fantasize, and they can try out many different ways of lovemaking. The best part of the relationship is that they never bore each other.

Gemini and Cancer

Mercury and the Moon are the rulers here, and there is delight between Gemini and Cancer, if not passion. Gemini changes his mind so frequently, and Cancer changes her moods so frequently, that they can understand if one person wants to play with sex toys one night and then prefers plain old sex the next. At the core of this relationship, Gemini is usually too cool for sentimental Cancer, but before these signs find that out, they can have a very good time.

Gemini and Leo

There are many opportunities for pleasure here. Gemini entertains Leo, who loves the drama of Gemini's different roles. These two take turns intriguing, servicing, and enjoying each other, and Gemini's air fans Leo's fire. Leo is a dramatic sign and always welcomes communication in any form. Gemini's verbal facility and love of wordplay will lead her to compliment Leo, and the fastest way into Leo's pants is with compliments. This combination is fun and hot. Both signs are inventive and like making love near a sunny beach.

Gemini and Virgo

This is called a square relationship in astrology, and it is not easy. Both Gemini and Virgo are ruled by Mercury and are thinking signs. However, they are in different and incompatible elements: air and earth.

> **When Stars Align**
> The best advice for Gemini is this: if you have the
> hots for Virgo, don't keep him waiting. He won't give
> you another chance.

Whereas airy Gemini and earthy Taurus interest
each other, Virgo and Gemini cannot meet in a manner
that encourages good sex. They may pique each other's
minds, but getting down to physical passion requires
naked lust. These two signs have too much going on
mentally and might not really get down to it. Sex between the two is interesting but not juicy.

Gemini and Libra

These two air signs always have lots to say to each
other. They are good friends, and that ease can turn
into friendly sex. Gemini is definitely the wilder of the
pair and may have to soothe Libra's need for romance
before there is any action.

> **When Stars Align**
> The scent of lavender will be a great turn-on for
> Gemini and Libra. And flowers or a favorite gift for
> Libra make the mood right.

Libra and Gemini both will enjoy sexy clothing. Libra
has no problem with thigh-high boots or thongs, and
Gemini will enjoy taking them off. Or another night,
they might indulge in cosplay with leather or lace de-

pending on the fantasy of the moment. Of course, all these games require lots of discussion, and that pleases both signs.

Gemini and Scorpio

Here we have the elements air and water, and a combination between the most easily distracted sign, Gemini, and the most focused sign, Scorpio. Sexually, it can work only because Gemini is able to experiment with anything that may pique Scorpio's interest. If Gemini wants games, that's okay with Scorpio. If Scorpio wants a brief encounter in a bathroom or behind the bushes, that's okay with Gemini. But at the end of the day, these two signs may not have much to do with each other once the games lose their excitement.

Gemini and Sagittarius

These are opposite signs, but they have compatible elements, air and fire. These opposites attract and complement each other. In the bedroom, both signs believe in fun and silliness. Emphasize any kind of oral sex with a Sag or Gemini, and both will be pleased. Love of sports and the outdoors gets the circulation and passion going with this sexy combination. One of their great pluses is that Gemini's natural inclination toward change and Sag's absolute need for motion and freedom have free reign when these two get together. They understand each other's needs, and that usually translates into good sex.

Gemini and Capricorn

This is a not-so-hot combination, unless each person has a bit of Gemini or Capricorn in the chart. The elements are air and earth, but Capricorn's sensuality and seriousness overwhelms Gemini's need to play and try out different sexual ideas. Also, Gemini rarely can be the kind of solid citizen that Capricorn enjoys, so these two might never get to first base. If they do and Gemini makes Capricorn laugh, then there is a possibility of a good time in the sack for a while.

When Stars Align

To help focus Gemini's hyper brain, try this technique. While both of you are lying on the floor, cup your Gemini's head in your hands and, with gentle pressure over the ears, cradle her head. You will notice her breathing immediately steady and relax. She might not like it for a long time, but it will prime her for relaxed sex.

Gemini and Aquarius

This combination can be the *Kama Sutra* in action because both signs are interested in exploring sex. They may have a great time belonging to an adult book club just to see what people are doing. The two air signs have compatible sexual energies. Passion, feeling, and love are not what bring these two together. Their combo is hot because they are mentally attuned and fearless in trying whatever sexy thing they think up. Each sign also understands the variable needs of the other and can give them space to fool around. They are good companions and will try to understand each other in and out of bed.

Gemini and Pisces

Air and water in this combination is not so hot. Gemini and Pisces have a square relationship, which is challenging for an in-depth connection. Sexually, Gemini's planet, Mercury, is too abrupt and fickle for Pisces's Neptunian sensitivity and emotional needs. Their rhythms are quite different, also, because Gemini is speedy and Pisces likes a languid time in the bedroom. Gemini may enjoy Pisces's dreaminess for a short time, but Pisces wants to shut off the mind in sex and Gemini wants to stimulate it. The two don't have enough in common energetically to produce hot sex.

Sex Planets: Mars and Venus

To learn more about yourself and your partner, find out where Venus and Mars are located in your or your partner's chart. Knowing this position will give you even more information about what he or she finds hot and exciting.

Mars in Gemini

This placement gives a person great intellectual force and curiosity. Communication abilities, both sexually and verbally, are very strong. There will be a strong fantasy life with this placement, and usually the person will have few inhibitions about making fantasy reality. Mars in Gemini can be assertive when he feels he knows a lot about the subject at hand. He might take a course in sexual techniques or read lots of books on the subject. When he feels confident, he will have no problem pursuing his intentions. If your partner has this position in his chart, emphasize learning about sex and how much you can learn together. Men with this position will tend to want more than one go-around per night. The first is almost like a tease, then there is a solid second act, and sometimes, a whopper of a finale.

Venus in Gemini

People with this placement are witty, can rhyme almost anything easily, and love to display their verbal prowess. A conversation with multiple partners is one of Venus in Gemini's sexual delights. The energy exchanged by talking caresses her mind and gives her a charge. A steady diet of only talk may not be enjoyable, but as a prelude or when there is no one else around, a verbal tryst is almost as good as the real thing. Because of the curiosity of Venus in Gemini, she may make dates with a partner's sister or brother or good friend, not realizing that this usually is not done! She can compartmentalize, and if she sees someone who catches her eye, she doesn't think, "Oh, this person is off-limits." Gemini does rule brothers and sisters, so it is all part of the wonderful world of sexual possibilities for this very flirtatious placement.

Chapter 4

Cancer
(June 21–July 22)

Cancer, the first cardinal water sign of the zodiac, can be a puzzling sign. As a cardinal sign that begins at the summer solstice, Cancerians are leaders, but they lead indirectly and are masters of innuendo and sly sexual clues. The sign's ruler is the Moon, which influences the ocean's tides. Familiarize yourself with the lunar cycle, and you will have the inside track on a Cancer's highs and lows. She is motherly and cranky; nurturing and selfish; humorous and moody; highly sexed, and then quickly turned off if something frightens or disturbs her.

The Nurturer

Nurturing sex may sound boring and remind you of eating your vegetables when you were young. But with a Cancerian partner, nurturing means fulfilling; not only do you get a good, sensitive sexual experience, but you also gain the feeling of cozy comfort akin to smelling cookies baking when you were a child. Cancer nurtures and protects, and a partner feels safe getting physical with Cancer. You may go crazy from his Moon-driven moodiness, but when it comes to doing the deed, Cancer offers a banquet of sensations because he is so responsive.

Written in the Stars

Cancer has an acute sense of smell. She particularly loves floral scents, such as narcissus, white lily, and jasmine. Make sure, wherever you have your hot date, that there are no bad smells from either cooking or refuse. It is an immediate turnoff.

A mother nurtures to make her children grow healthy and strong. In the bedroom, Cancerians nurture either to get good sex or to begin building a home together that includes good sex. Cancer is acutely aware of offering something in order to reap the rewards. His concerns for partners and caretaking are sincere but not altruistic. A Cancerian expects you to intuit exactly what he wants and gets very cranky when you prove not to be a mind reader. Then he turns on the guilt.

The symbol of Cancer is the Crab, and the crab sidles forward and backward and then progresses slowly forward. The crab also carries her home on her back, and penetrating a Cancerian's shell is half the game in a sexy encounter.

Crabs are land and sea creatures, and this amphibious nature is another of Cancer's quirks. She longs to swim in oceans of feeling but snaps to attention at the demands of the practical earth. Nostalgic yearning is part of her romantic and sexual charm. The sweetness that Cancerians have will not show at the first meeting or first fling. There may be lots of feeling and hot sexual action, but the true expression of Cancer's sexuality takes a while to develop and always requires making love in a homey environment.

What Turns Cancer On—and Off

The first great turn-on for Cancer is where sex happens. Cancerians are turned on by everything that happens in the home. Out on the street, she may seem closed off and even fearful. If you ask a Cancerian outside of her nest what she thinks of such-and-such sexual practice, she may very well say she is not in favor of it. But in the bedroom or on the living room couch—that good old comfortable place that has held fantasies and comforts for so long—anything can happen. Anything that reminds her of a childhood home is also a great turn-on. Wear a perfume or aftershave that reminds her of one of her parents, and the seduction is complete. Sex for Cancerians is associated with having a family—symbolically or literally—and Cancer loves to be surrounded by family. This is a sexy feeling for Cancer because it ensures that she will never be lonely.

Cancer is totally turned on by soft skin. Cancer's own skin is extremely sensitive and must be protected from the cold and the sun. Cancer loves feeling soft, smooth skin, and may pay particular attention to a partner's complexion. Cancerians enjoy a clean look even in the sexy areas.

Passion Points

Cancer is the only sign in the zodiac besides Scorpio that physically rules a traditional erogenous zone, in this case the breasts. All the associations with comfort, abundance, and sex that breasts have are part of a Cancerian's sexual personality.

Cancerians like classic styles that are unambiguously male or female. Underwear for women should be frilly and lacy, and men prefer underwear in cotton or silk—white, navy blue, or charcoal. Too many different sensations while getting dressed in the morning can overload Cancer's sensory equipment and make him confused.

Turnoffs for Cancer are unexpected, quick sexual liaisons in anonymous places. In fact, it would be unlikely for this to happen. Cancer may look longingly at someone at a party or business function, entertain the idea of a quickie, and exercise all his power to get the message across that he is interested, but he prefers getting to know a person first and then making love.

> **Written in the Stars**
> The full moon is the most likely time to expect any wild sexual behavior. Usually Cancer is conservative with sex, but he feels especially vibrant and sensitive at this time. However, if you are beginning a fling with Cancer, you will have better luck starting at the new moon.

Another turnoff is a partner who comes on too strong. A Cancer man is intimidated by this approach and uncomfortable because he is not in the lead. And Cancerian women do not thrill to this form of seduction. They are too sensitive and enjoy romance too much to favor a blunt sexual pass in which there is no finesse. Multiple partners, or any kind of orgiastic sexual activity, is another turnoff. Cancer has the libido to enjoy this, but there are too many unfamiliar vibrations to make it satisfying. One-on-one is the best approach.

Cancer's Strengths and Specialties

Cancer is the only sign besides Scorpio that rules a traditional erogenous zone, the breasts. Women feel sexy and proud of their boobs, and their partners love to caress and touch them. Men also have very sensitive breasts and will love special attention paid to their nipples. Breasts serve double duty in the Cancerian view of sex—they are sexy and nurturing. A child sucks for food, and a partner for pleasure. What a great invention! A male Cancerian will know just the right touch for his partner's chest, and a Cancerian woman will be very responsive when her partner knows the right way to handle her breasts.

Passion Points

Cancer also rules the stomach. Rubbing tummies and gentle kisses there may be the best prelude to a night of hot, good sex.

The symbol for Cancer looks suspiciously like 69. Traditionally, the symbol denoted the breasts, but it also clearly has a connotation of another pleasurable activity that Cancerians love. This particular position is definitely a good choice for your Cancer partner. Everyone is nurtured and pleasured at the same time, and the bodies fit well together.

Cancer's Weaknesses and Foibles

The fussy factor is a Cancerian weakness. If things don't feel quite right in the bedroom or he has had a bad day, it is difficult for him to change gears. The only remedy is a bath and/or alone time. This is tough if you have your heart set on a sexy evening, but if you can be patient, the Crab will emerge in a better mood and ready for sex.

Weaknesses also involve athletic, challenging sex. Cancer's problem is not that he lacks libido but that anything rough or overtly kinky startles him, and he feels he can't be at his best. There is a very traditional streak in most Cancerians, and they do not like to experiment unless they are absolutely sure it will work. Introduce innovation slowly and Cancer will get the knack, but Cancer builds up confidence from past successes. If something does not go well the first time out, then it is usually crossed off the list and will not be attempted again.

Written in the Stars

Cancer partners must learn from their own experiences. He will not appreciate sex manuals or instructional DVDs. Looking at other people having sex infringes on his sense of uniqueness. Erotic films or pictures, however, will definitely stimulate him, as Cancerians are very visual people. They can imitate anything they see and like.

You may assume that, as a water sign, Cancer likes to make love in the shower or the pool. This is not always true. Water is the element of emotions, and with a watery environment in conjunction with Cancer's naturally fluid emotions, there could be too much of a good thing. Cancerian women don't feel quite solid in these situations, and Cancerian men may become so relaxed that they can't rise to the occasion.

The Cancer Man

Cancer is a feminine sign and the sign of the Great Mother. The Cancer man is usually very connected to his feminine side and is rarely into conquer-and-dominate kinds of sex. He wants a partner to follow his lead for mutual pleasure, but his lead is more like a gentle invitation. You will find one of the most appealing parts of his personality in his lunar laugh. This unmistakable and often uncontrollable laugh ebbs and flows with the lunar cycle. It reflects his wonderful sense of humor, and the ability to tell stories and humor himself out of blue moods. Laughter almost always precedes sex for the Cancer man.

A Cancerian's masculine side is frequently more intellectual than physical. He loves history, reading, and music. Frequently, he is an avid collector of books, antiques, or anything that seizes his historical imagination.

He is also usually very astute about money and accumulates it easily, but is not keen about parting with it without good reason. In the seduction phase of a relationship, a Cancer man is very generous. He wants to show his date a good time and feel important and potent with how much he can spend. If the relationship moves toward a commitment, and Cancerian men are definitely the marrying kind, the household budget will be important to maintain. It's best not to talk about money matters until way after sex. Sometimes, Cancer men don't know what to do with their possessive feelings. However, Cancer men can be charmed out of any of their tightfisted attitudes with a smile and a few tears. If he sees that something is distressing his partner, he wants to rectify it. Emotional distress reminds the Cancerian man of his own very sentimental and emotional side, and he will go to lengths to avoid showing that to a partner at first.

Written in the Stars
Give your Cancer man time to get used to any gift of clothing, such as a sweater or shirt. He will sniff around it, try it on, maybe leave it in the tissue paper for a while, and then decide he loves it and wear it frequently. Choose nighttime colors such as gray, black and white, navy blue, and black.

The idea of a sex buddy or a friend with benefits goes against the grain of a Cancer man. It is all too quick and too flashy for him to feel comfortable. Cancer likes history and wants to have a history with a person before he exposes himself physically. His quiet confidence blooms in relationships.

Before he picks a partner for life, Cancer may dabble in what the French call *amour de la boue*, or "love of the mud." This is a brief tour through the more risqué and kinky areas of loving. The motivation here is curiosity; once a Cancerian man passes through this phase, it is finished. If this appeals to you, catch the male Crab during this phase without any thought of a future relationship, and you probably will have a good time. It is unusual for a Cancerian man to make a commitment solely on the basis of hot sex.

As mentioned before, the moon influences all Cancerians. A Cancer man will be hot to trot at the full moon and ready to explore the outer reaches of his sexual personality.

The Cancer Woman

The lunar emphasis in a Cancerian woman reveals itself in a very feminine vulnerability that is also fiercely protective. She can be a hotshot businesswoman who cooks every night, or a scholarly type lost in the historical past. Whatever her profession or work is, having sex is almost always within the context of a relationship. One-night stands and sex on a whim are not usual. She invests too much of her sensitivity in making love.

Sex for a Cancer woman usually includes sympathy and good food. Taking care of a partner turns her on. This is not only to please, but also because it makes her own sexual juices flow. She likes orgasms just fine, but is much more excited by her partner's release. It is a mark of surrender and intimacy for her.

As a water sign, Cancerian women feel relaxed and sexy near the water. Surprisingly, they may not like to be *in* water. She can feel waterlogged when she spends a long time in the ocean, and if the surf is rough, Cancer is not happy. Fighting the waves is the opposite of what feels good to her.

Cancerian women are not big on adventurous sex. This is a sexy sign of the zodiac, but sensitivity and innate modesty preclude riotous, wild behavior. If her partner is into something new or risky, the Cancer woman will follow along and may even feel thrilled at the prospect, but usually she won't initiate anything unusual. It would also be unlikely for a Cancer girl to do anything sexual in a semipublic space. The very thought of being seen or interrupted would freeze her cold.

Setting the Scene

Maybe there is a special cottage in the woods beside a brook, with wisteria growing all around, which has been in your family for ages. You are walking in the woods and come upon the cottage and go in to take a look. There is a large bed with a skylight directly over it. The cottage feels like it could be from any historical period, but its major feature is that it is protected and charming. There is a kitchen with a full refrigerator, and effortlessly you whip up a beautiful dinner. The moon is rising now, and strangely enough, the beams shine exactly on the bed. While the dishes are waiting in the sink, the crickets chirp, and you hear the sound of the brook lapping at the shores through the open windows.

Written in the Stars

Nurturing for a Cancerian woman also means she will invest time thinking about how you will get to her place, how you will get home, whether there will be bad traffic at a certain time, and what other dangers you might meet on the road—in short, anything that might inhibit the very sexy time that Cancer envisions. She will want you to call her before and after your date. If she doesn't call you herself, it usually signifies no more sex for you two.

The time is right for the tide of sexiness that has been swelling throughout the day. Maybe there is a little tease while taking off the hiking boots you have been wearing. That moon is so bright now that there is no other choice for you and your Cancerian partner but to hit the soft white percale sheets and imagine you are every couple in history—from Cleopatra and Mark Antony to Napoleon and Josephine. Why not? The body remembers pleasure for centuries.

Sexy Matches: The Hot and Not-So-Hot Combinations

Since Cancer is one of the most sentimental signs of the zodiac, if he connects with someone who is on the not-so-hot list, he may continue the relationship because of past history. Perhaps that not-so-hot Aquarius and Cancer have had a good time in the past. Or perhaps Cancer wants to stick together longer because things might change. Cancer should always follow his feelings.

Cancer and Aries

Both these signs are leadership signs, but in very different ways and elements. Cancer is a water sign, and Aries is a fire sign. In this case, the combo is not so hot, because Cancer needs flow and consistency, and Aries needs quick changes and swift moves. If aggressive tension and anger fuel their sexuality, sometimes this combo can be hot for an experiment. Aries might learn a few things from the Cancerian charm and sensitivity. After a while, though, Cancer's emotionality rains on Aries's parade.

Cancer and Taurus

Water and earth have good opportunities together for sex, friendship, and long-term partnership. Their rulers, the Moon and Venus, respectively, are interested in harmonious relationships and will work hard to perfect sex. This is a fertile and sensual combination; after all, earth and water are all that flowers need to grow. They both need to feel secure: Cancer cares about emotional security, and Taurus is concerned with material security. This is a definite hot connection because the two signs feel safe and sexy with each other. Both signs also love the feel of soft skin, good food, and a comfortable home.

Cancer and Gemini

The Moon and Mercury together in the elements of water and air are okay. Cancer can be wacky but is always rooted in her feelings. Gemini is wacky and experimental, because he thinks up different positions or sexual fantasies. Cancer may at first indulge in Gemini's quick-change artistry, but then she begins to get restless and senses that the variety is not based on feelings. Then the Gemini charm begins to feel cold to Cancer, and she yearns for a steadier stream of feeling and sex. This is a good choice for a fun short-term relationship, but may be too erratic for Cancer long term.

Cancer and Cancer

There is no place like home, and home is where these two Crabs love to be. Sexually speaking, they are content to hole up in the bedroom for a night. They will mirror each other's sexual needs and both feel very satisfied. The challenge may come the next morning when one has to go out of the house (which neither of these homebodies will be inclined to do). This combo is rarely interested in just a fling. Both signs look for a long-term sexual relationship and will not get involved when there is not some promise of that on the horizon.

Cancer and Leo

Here we have the Moon and the Sun, which represent two ancient and archetypal female and male principles: the mother and the father. Cancer loves the paternal dimension of Leo's generous character because it feels family-like, and Leo laps up the nurturing attention that Cancer offers so easily. This is a good sexual affair and relationship. Long term, the difference in their elements, water and fire, may fizzle, but if there is enough history together, Cancer will make it work.

When Stars Align

The sweetness of Cancer's personality belies a formidable anger when he is spurned. Cancer always makes his feelings known, and if he feels mistreated, he will not be quiet about making you know his discontent. His typical passive aggressive mood becomes clearly aggressive because you have committed a Cancerian mortal sin: broken a bond between you.

Cancer and Virgo

Water and earth are a friendly, sexy vibration between two people. Here, the Moon and Mercury are mildly hot. The Moon is emotional, and Mercury is cooler but sensual. They are not terrifically passionate, because Cancer feels constricted by Virgo's precise and analytical tendencies. And woe to the couple if Cancer feels criticized; this situation marks the end of sexual possibilities. This is a nice combo, very respectful of each other. A relationship between these two won't light up the sky, but neither will it harm anyone.

Cancer and Libra

Astrologically, this traditionally challenging relationship has a lot going for it. It is a hot combination because both signs melt into romance and believe in the specialness of coupledom. Cancer loves Libra's sexy beauty. Also, the nurturing part of the Cancerian character usually includes hospitality, and there is not a better aphrodisiac for Libra than entertaining. After-a-party sex in a beautiful home that both Libra and Cancer like is not only sexy, but also promises to move the relationship forward into a long-term partnership. These two signs can argue fiercely because they are passionate about their points of view. But sometimes, make-up-after-an-argument sex is the best, and Cancer and Libra can take advantage of that.

Cancer and Scorpio

The Moon and Mars in the same element, water, make this a hot combination. There is a wordless connection between these two signs, where they both know that in a very few minutes, hours, or days, they will be off to sexual-pleasure land. Cancer may be the more conservative partner, but the flow of sexy moods between her and Scorpio can melt inhibitions and lead her to explore a few areas that she might not usually try. Cancer may enjoy dominance-and-submission fantasies with Scorpio for a while. However, if Scorpio dominates too much, the Crab will scuttle away because she feels her sensitivities are not coddled. Before Cancer leaves, though, these two will have had a very good time between the sheets.

Cancer and Sagittarius

Water and fire in this case fizzle rather than boil. Cancer's sexiness depends on a feeling of emotional security for the moment, and Sagittarius is not into the prelude to lovemaking that Cancer needs. Cancer wants closeness, and implicit in that desire is the possibility of a relationship continuing. Sag feels the Crab's pincers and says, "Get me out of here." If Cancer is very young and feeling bold, a relationship between the two is exciting, and there is no other zodiacal combination that can laugh together so well. Long term, these two live life with different expectations and will usually pass each other by.

Cancer and Capricorn

These are opposite signs, with water and earth as the elements. This is a hot combo because it fulfills both signs' deepest needs. Cancer feels secure, and Capricorn feels nurtured and entertained. Capricorn will never fear that Cancer is a gold digger, because Cancer always wants more than money and status. Between the sheets, the emotional flow of sexy feelings truly can melt Capricorn's stubbornness and tensions. In other words, Cancer helps Capricorn lighten up. Traditionally, Capricorn has symbolized the father, and Cancer the mother. This fundamental polarity is a hot connection.

Cancer and Aquarius

This is a not-so-hot combination. Cancer is too emotional to tolerate the dispassionate friendliness that Aquarius offers to his friends and partners. If Aquarius is going through one of his turned-off phases, Cancer will take it personally and feel abandoned. Once in a blue moon, these two might get it on, but that isn't usual, satisfying, or long-lasting.

Cancer and Pisces

The Moon and Neptune are the planets involved in this combination, and both signs are in the element of water. It is a sexy combination in its own way. Hot means sparks, and these two signs are more into merging and highly emotional sex. Physically, they share a love of subtlety, groove on stimulants, and retreat from the world to create a pleasure nest. Cancer and Pisces together can create infinite fantasy variations that keep them occupied and cooing for a long time. Cancer will work hard to create a love nest for the Crab and the Fish so they may enjoy each other's sensitivities.

> **Passion Points**
>
> The soft skin under the upper arm has a delectable feel in Cancer women. Caressing this area feels especially intimate. From there, the breasts are not far away.

Sex Planets: Mars and Venus

Find out where Mars and Venus are for you and your partner to deepen your understanding of you both. Whenever a planet is in the sign of Cancer, the planet is sensitized and interested in feelings.

Mars in Cancer

Mars in Cancer has been called a position of *divine discontent*. The world and people as they are irritate a person when Mars is in Cancer. He can't stand crowds, is sensitive to weather changes, and cannot bear rejection of any sort. Watery and sensitive, Cancer is not an easy position for fiery Mars energy. However, if you examine the charts of many of our greatest artists and writers, you will find Mars in Cancer. Think of a beautiful pearl that forms from a grain of sand irritating the oyster. The irritation is the source of his creativity.

However, this sign is very sexy as he goes through life trying to feel comfortable. His unpredictability and sensual disposition toward life make him a responsive and surprising partner. He cannot be direct about his sexual desires or needs. To discover what technique, romantic setting, or position will intrigue him, listen if he talks about sex. He is not consciously giving you clues, but a word to the wise is sufficient. Mars in Cancer can be a difficult placement, but remember that the sweet meat of a crab is under his shell, and it takes some work to get at it.

Venus in Cancer

Venus, the sign of love and beauty, is harmonious when she is in the feminine sign of Cancer. Her home life is an art, and no hot date is complete without a home-cooked meal. These people are easily sympathetic and will listen avidly to your sexual desires and fantasies. When one seems appealing to her, then the experimenting begins. Her motivation may come more from a desire to please than overflowing passion.

Venus in Cancer tends to give a person a sentimental side that looks for emotional security in sexual relations. Without that appeal, Venus in Cancer is affectionate rather than hot. This can be a very playful position because Venus in Cancer easily recalls her childhood, when games were always fun.

Chapter 5

Leo
(July 23–August 22)

The second fire sign of the zodiac,
Leo is one of the powerhouse signs. His
personality is outsized and generous, and he
roars with delight at all sexual activity. He is
king of the jungle and finds safaris (that is,
being on the lookout for partners) intriguing,
whether on city streets or in the countryside.
The ruling planet of Leo is the Sun (which
caresses us all), and there is no happier
sign than Leo when his sexual heat
burns as brightly as the sun.

The Dramatist

Leo is like a lion in terms of protecting his territory and ruling over his subjects, and he hopes no one notices his soft spot: insecurity. He can feel very diminished if he is not receiving enough attention, and he works hard to stay in the spotlight. The Greek myth of Phaeton is interesting for Leos both in and out of bed. Phaeton wanted to drive the sun chariot of his father, Helios. His father refused him because the job was too difficult for an inexperienced boy. But Phaeton insisted. He drove too close to the sun, scorched the land and himself, and was quickly killed by Zeus's thunderbolt. Mature Leo knows how to share his solar energy sexually; immature Leo burns up and agitates for attention and can thoroughly turn off any prospective partners.

> **Written in the Stars**
> Shower Leo with compliments, and you will not have to do anything else to lead her to the bedroom.

Big loves, big desires, and big affection are the dramatic strokes that lead Leo in the sexual arena. She likes to feel in command of her stage and plays many roles with her partners. If you have a favorite dramatic sex scenario, then Leo is the partner for you. Playing king/queen and loyal subject would be a favorite, with many encores. Some Leos can be very exhibitionistic and enjoy sex in less-than-private spaces.

Leo's generosity is real, and it truly gives him pleasure to bring you pleasure. At first, he may focus only on his own pleasure, but Leo is a hospitable sign and will not want his partner to leave unsatisfied or unhappy. Leo will also be dramatic when he's dissatisfied. He may only hint about it to you, but if you don't pick up the hints, there will not be a repeat engagement of lovemaking. Leo is writing his own play and needs partners who are willing to be both a character and an audience. Follow-the-leader (with Leo as leader) is his preferred style, but he may play at following…sometimes.

What Turns Leo On—and Off

Leo is turned on by attention: undivided, direct, and unwavering. Don't take phone calls when you are with her, eliminate interruptions in the bedroom, and maintain eye contact during intimate moments. Leo likes to see as well as feel. Leo is also turned on by the drama of the entire sexual experience. She doesn't like to compartmentalize: first do this, next that, and then finish up with such and such. Leo's passion leads and dictates whether there are kisses all over the body and then you get together, or maybe the feeling is so strong that there are no preliminaries, and you go for the gold immediately. Every time you get physical, there will be a different springboard to sex.

A major turn-on for Leo is being with someone who is generous. If you are a stingy type, hide it if you want to score with Leo. A Leo leaves big tips whether or not he is wealthy. Being free with money makes him feel good and powerful. Leo also prefers a glamorous lifestyle, with flashy clothes and top-notch accessories. He requires a partner who can rise to any social occasion. Half of Leo's seduction strategy is scooping up the king or queen of the ball and then showing them how life can be even better with a Leo.

Turnoffs are people who are halfhearted and don't approach life and sex with their all. Leo doesn't mind if a few things don't work out, but reticence and wimpiness frustrate her and snuff out her enthusiasm. Leo doesn't like to supply all the energy or coax someone into having a good time. She will and can lead, but her partner must be a worthy follower. Leo loves images and is very status-conscious. She may fall for someone who suits her image of a good partner and be disappointed when they fall short of expectations. The packaging can be more important than the contents. But Leo still demands good and fashionable packaging.

Written in the Stars

Leo's hair may be her prized possession. Stroke it, brush it, caress it, buy grooming products for it, and watch out if she says it is a bad hair day—then the whole day, and perhaps night, she will not be happy. She will either need sex to console her or be in such a funk that nothing but ice cream will help.

Leo's Strengths and Specialties

Leo's greatest strength may be his daring with all sexual encounters. Whichever way passion leads, he will go there. Innately, Leo is not particularly kinky, and he will eschew slave-master scenarios. He knows that he is the leader and does not need to role-play. He is athletic and very responsive to temperature. He tends to run hot, and will enjoy lovemaking in the heat. It's all fire to him. Daring for Leo means having sex in public places, teasing, and casting meaningful glances in inappropriate settings, the last two of which may lead both people to hide for a bit, with lots of seductive moves and suggestions before getting down to it.

Although Leo usually likes a glamorous partner and is very impressed by exciting, worldly accomplishments, she will take a chance on a diamond in the rough if her libido is piqued. Also, Leo enjoys partners who are younger than she is. The guiding and educating role is a natural one for her in all areas of life, and when pleasure is involved, she naturally gravitates to leading the way.

The area of the body ruled by Leo is the heart, and for Leo, this means ardor and passion that is not phony. This sign believes in truth of expression. Lovemaking, no matter how long the relationship lasts, comes from the heart. Leo will be petulant and wounded if you doubt his sincerity. He will also not cotton to a partner who is superficial. Playing games is delightful for Leo, but they must be backed up by feeling and intensity.

Leo's Weaknesses and Foibles

Leo holds tension in her back, and if she is worried or not sure that the relationship is going to work out, she will feel stiffness there. Massage or a little bit of dirty dancing just to make things dramatic will limber her up. Leo does not require romance, as Libra does, but it won't hurt.

The greatest weakness in Leo's sexual character is the tendency to monopolize his partner's attention. He wants to receive pleasure and the complete attention of his partner. He is generous and will want you to feel satisfied also, but if he doesn't feel your approval and applause 100 percent for the magnificent experience he has just given you, he will deflate, pout, and be very testy. Leo is never overtly angry, but his pride is formidable, and anything that affects performance will undoubtedly be your fault. Lots of ego stroking is needed here. After some time and experience together, Leo will turn off the roaring pride and begin to trust, but like the lions who circle each other, vying for the lionesses' attention, Leo wants to know for this encounter that he is your one and only.

As a partner, Leo, for all her exhibitionist tendencies, can be very self-conscious, especially if she has worries about looks or body type. It will take a long time for her to uncover what she doesn't like about herself. Sexually, it may not affect her performance, but as a mark of intimacy, it might take her a while to get comfortable. Even with some self-consciousness, Leo is very honest about how the orgasm experience turns out. She won't criticize you or feel diminished if things weren't so hot, because there will always be another chance...and it could be that very night.

☀ Written in the Stars

Leo men like to wear jewelry such as cuff links, tie tacks, gold bracelets, and perhaps a gold chain. He might also wear an earring. Make sure the jewelry is gold. Leos do not care for silver or even platinum. If you want to please him, consider giving any of these as gifts.

The Leo Man

Leo is a masculine sign and usually very virile. The men are good-looking and are sexy because they are caring, protective people. A Leo man has a courtly deference to his partner. He is gallant and only sorry that today's fashions do not include swirling cloaks and a plumed hat for him to doff in front of whomever he fancies. The gesture is all-important with the Leo man. As a partner, he will want his mate to look good and be very self-possessed. He is not interested in weepy emotions and sentimentality. All that water puts out his fire, and he mistrusts it.

The Leo man is playful, and if he starts jumping on the bed and bouncing you along with him, he wants you to play too. Once you are both reclining, Leo will lavish attention on all parts of his partner's body. This undertaking will be accompanied with appreciative smacking noises and lots of fun. When approaching sensitive areas, he will appreciate knowing that he has found the right spot. Try moans and purrs rather than words. Leo understands nonverbal satisfaction very well.

Leo has a big ego and needs attention. He wants to know he is the best, and if you throw in numerous compliments about the size, elegance, and beauty of his penis, you will bring out the best in him.

The Leo Woman

The Leo woman can be a prima donna and very seductive and choosy about her partners. She will check and then check again to make sure that connecting with that certain someone will enhance her image. This is not a mental process, but instinct. Female Leos do not want anyone with less verve than they have. The Leo woman enjoys a partner who is macho, but she doesn't mind vulnerability. If you make the first move, then you pay for the date. She will return the invitation and be happy to treat, but don't try splitting the bill. It smacks of the ordinary for Leos, and they hate that.

In the bedroom, watch the contented Leo woman become a purring kitten. If she is really turned on, she becomes a wildcat, scratching and love biting and acting slightly out of control. She is passionate, and if she finds a match, she will let it all hang out. She may not be as experimental in bed as other signs, but the quality of her sexual expression and what she generously offers to her partner more than make up for the lack of any strange experimenting.

Written in the Stars

Leo women are very concerned with their appearance, and dress for delight and seduction. They are usually very good-looking and like emphasizing their breasts and bottoms—which they work hard to keep firm and appealing. Their style is flashy, and they love wearing jewelry.

Setting the Scene

Basking in a warm, sunny place with a hibiscus flower behind one ear, Leo prowls for the perfect spot for sex. It could be outdoors, indoors in a luxurious room, in the back of a swank limousine, or in the corner office on the twenty-fourth floor with the perfect view.

Wherever Leo gets together, the setting must be posh and as luxe as possible. Orange flower water on the sheets or a tryst in the private patio hammock will encourage Leo's passion. Leo is athletic enough to manage sex on any kind of furniture. Switch on the lamp, open the blinds, or, at night, light lots of candles. Leo likes to see the beauty and pleasure that await. If your private date follows going out and being seen by friends and people who admire you, it will add zest to sex.

The first move for Leo is loving the mane. With a few well-chosen compliments, followed by brushing and caressing hair, you may not need much more to invite hot and enjoyable sex. The early morning and late night are both prime times for Leo. Start lying side-by-side, and then, if your Leo partner is male, consider letting him dominate. Leo women, on the other hand, are kittens in bed and may expect the first move to come from their partners. Wherever you are, have a robe available for your partner, one monogrammed with the Superman logo or with the Wonder Woman logo. There is no doubt that these robes will encourage the famous Leo ego to be at its best. Enjoy!

Sexy Matches: The Hot and Not-So-Hot Combinations

If one of the not-so-hot combos has caught your fancy, don't despair: Leo's passion, ardor, and fire may very well transform a relationship that classically is not hot into an experience that knocks both your socks off.

Leo and Aries

No energy problems here. It's a combination of fire and fire, with Leo's star, the Sun, heating up Mars. These two signs have equal physical force, love to challenge each other, and can hold their own in any kind of sexual contest. They don't waste time on tedious preliminaries when passion calls. Leo will want more seduction than Aries and will be a little less impulsive, but together these two have a fine basis for a relationship. Emphasize athletic positions and encounters.

Leo and Taurus

Astrologically, this combination is considered challenging. Leo and Taurus are both fixed signs, enormously willful and very strong. If they spark each other's interest, they can have a dynamic time in bed. The operative word is *if*. Leo's fire needs more oomph and pizzazz than Taurus's earthy nature usually has to give. Leo offers fireworks and exciting scenarios, and Taurus, naked sensuality. One night at a party with a good deal of sangria may make this combo rock. In the cold dawn, Leo will chalk one up to experience and move on.

Leo and Gemini

Fire and air and a lot of laughs are shared between these two signs. The sex can be adventurous, with lots of oral stimulation, which Leo loves. A Gemini will happily serve a Leo, and that keeps Leo interested and rapturous. Leo likes a willing subject, but Gemini is not always dependable, and this may put Leo in a snit. This combo may easily restore their good humor and proceed to more pleasurable communication.

> **When Stars Align**
> A great aphrodisiac for your Leo is champagne and caviar. It may not be the actual food, but the lifestyle these luxuries represent, that will get her panting.

Leo and Cancer

These next-door-neighbor signs share one trait: they both love to be adored. If, as partners, they can switch roles and agree who gets the adoring today, the sexual combo can work. Leo is ruled by the Sun, and Cancer is ruled by the Moon. These celestial lights embody masculine protection and feminine nurturing principles, respectively, and Leo and Cancer may feel they owe it to themselves to explore this polarity. After a time, the elements of fire and water between these two signs wear on each other. If the relationship doesn't move into a romance and then a partnership, the sex will lose its kick.

Leo and Leo

In between each Leo's roar, there is hot sex and a lot of fun. But understand that both people are vying for the other's undivided attention. Unless one Leo likes to give attention because that is the way they feel sexiest (this is not very usual), these two cannot stand a low worshipping quotient for very long. In other words, although they communicate well in bed, their relationship usually resembles a competition and fizzles.

Leo and Virgo

Fire and earth are their respective elements, and although these two come from different worlds, Virgo soothes Leo's need for attention and adoration. Virgo is a service-oriented sign, and Leo loves to be serviced sexually, romantically, and personally. Leo fires Virgo's somewhat pedestrian imagination, and he loves the way Virgo puts herself together—the understated, classy look. Leo can feel his insecurities have protection when Virgo is around, as she is likely to feel insecure too. Because of Virgo's flexibility, this combination can work; then, Leo gets to be the star.

Leo and Libra

Fire and air and a love of romance and sexual drama bring these two signs together. Their sex life is hot, and usually they are both so good-looking that they attract each other easily. With the Sun (Leo) shining on Venus (Libra), there are infinite opportunities for sexy connections. Leo is the more adventuresome partner, but has such style that Leo may lead Libra into situations, positions, and practices that Libra never imagined. Leo makes Libra feel comfortable and a little naughty at the same time. This is a hot, winning combo.

Leo and Scorpio

What to say? These two fixed signs have the astrological challenge of being square to each other. In astrological terms, that means that they do not come together; however, in sexual terms, they may come together just hunky-dory because each gets off on the other's sexiness. They are powerhouse signs, and Leo will enjoy trying to get Scorpio to acknowledge his majesty. Leo is overt and Scorpio is covert, and exploring all the ramifications of this duality makes for hot, intense, unusual, passionate sex. Sex in every position, oral sex, and sex toys are all possible with these two warriors. Out of the bedroom, these signs may not have anything in common and may quarrel about everything. If an argument is a prelude to sex, it will fuel both partners, but if it involves deciding which color the couch should be, it becomes extremely tiring.

Leo and Sagittarius

Fire and fire and the Sun and Jupiter rule these signs, respectively, and make this combination hot and openhearted. Together, they have good-natured sex free from insecurities, and much contact with the darker side of each person's nature. Both of these fire signs are very physical and enjoy athletic sex. The sole drawback for Leo is the Sagittarian tendency toward blunt comments. Leo needs compliments to get and keep the motors going, and Sagittarius is incapable of glossing over what she sees as "the truth." So, when Sagittarius says, "Your hair looked better yesterday," she may not realize that it will take Leo a while to recover from this assault, and the result may mean no hanky-panky for a while.

Leo and Capricorn

The Sun and the Goat have issues. Some of them can be solved in the bedroom, and some will not ever go away. This fire and earth combination can get together because they both enjoy status, social functions, and the world of passion. There is solid sexual energy between these two, and a love of ambitious sex. Leo is more playful than Capricorn is and wants to fool around with foreplay before diving into the main event. The issue between these two is timing. Leo is quick, and Capricorn is slow. After a few weeks, the discrepancies here will become a drag and override the good sex that may have gotten these two people together in the first place. The good bank account/security issue is a powerful stimulant between Leo and Capricorn, but over time, Leo will not be able to shine brightly with Capricorn's serious character.

Leo and Aquarius

These two are powerfully attracted to each other and can be a hot and successful combination for the short term. Part of the charge is their very different expectations in life. Leo is all about me, and Aquarius is all about the group. As each sign woos the other to their way of thinking, they find lots to keep them busy in the bedroom. Leo works to get Aquarius to acknowledge her wonderfulness, and Aquarius works to capture Leo's fire, ardor, and warmth. They warm each other. When Aquarius brings other friends into the relationship, not necessarily sexually, Leo gets jealous and realizes that she is not the one and only. This is the point where the signs may agree to part. But in the meantime, they have fun.

Leo and Pisces

Leo likes Pisces's otherworldly, fantasy-oriented charm. The Fish's very elusiveness lures Leo into a hazy, romantic world that promises delights. Leo feels protective toward Pisces, and that brings out Pisces's more sensitive side, sexually speaking. This is a tender connection where Leo may not feel the need to prove anything because Pisces accepts Leo as is. Both signs enjoy wine and other stimulants. Pisces may require these to keep up with Leo, and over time, Leo will want a more solid, less emotional partner.

Sex Planets: Mars and Venus

To learn more about yourself and your partner, find out where Venus and Mars are located in your or your partner's chart. Knowing this position will give you even more information about what you and your partner find hot and exciting.

Mars in Leo

Energetic Mars is well placed in flashy, fiery Leo. People with this placement are born extroverts and enjoy making a big deal of everything they do. Seduction is a big deal, and sex is an even bigger deal. There may be a small tendency to exaggerate sexual prowess and success with this placement. They may boast of those they have bedded. This is all in the service of increasing importance and desirability. Mars in Leo does not mean this type must lie; they just like the feeling of being important.

> **Passion Points**
>
> Concentrate on the soft hair between the eyebrows or on a downy cheek. It's a subtle feeling, but one that Mars in Leo appreciates.

This placement loves mirrors. He checks himself out in every mirror he passes, enjoys special mirrors in the bedroom for visual enhancement, and may carry a pocket mirror in case insecurity threatens. The insecurity comes because of Mars in Leo's tendency to exaggerate. He loves mirrors because seeing his reflection grounds him and assures him that he is as good-looking and desirable as he believes himself to be. The good news for Mars in Leo is that the mirrors usually don't lie.

Venus in Leo

Men and women with this placement love beauty and the arts. They dream big and pay attention to their homes with an eye for beauty, and also to impress. Columns on the front porch or a gazebo in the backyard give Venus in Leo the feeling of the estate they feel they belong in. Sexually, these people are flirts and teases. Venus in Leo has a lot of pride, and it is wrapped up in sexual prowess and conquest. Playing around means giving rise to all manner of fantasy and wildness. She likes to dominate a sexual relationship until it gets serious. If the fling becomes a commitment, the women will become demure and kittenish, and the men almost Tarzan-like. A commitment means having a stake in society, and Venus in Leo wants that to be respectable.

Chapter 6

Virgo
(August 23–September 22)

Virgo is an earth sign and is ruled by the messenger god, Mercury. Virgo's message is that sex is good, healthy fun. The god Mercury also rules thought, and Virgo is a thinking sign. She may have to work hard to shut down the parade of annoyances that can plague her brain and interfere with passion, but Virgo understands that leaving details behind and plunging into a physical, nonanalytical sexual experience will be extremely satisfying.

The Perfectionist

Of all the earth signs, Virgo is the most flexible and enjoys different and changing sexual experiences. Think of the bounty of the earth, and you begin to have an idea of Virgo's sensuality and sexuality. Virgo, the Virgin, is tremendously interested in and responsive to sex. The virgin symbolism of the sign does not mean that she is untouchable and likes it that way, but that she seeks purity and perfection in every encounter that comes along. That means perfect sex, perfect technique, and perfect orgasms are a lifelong quest. Virgo may not find what she is looking for, but pursuit is the goal. After all, if something is perfect, then what do you have left to do—there is nothing else to work on! Virgo likes to work for everything, including pleasure. She will shop for sexy clothes, create a perfect spot for her trysts, and make sure her partner uses hypoallergenic soap because heavy scents offend her delicate senses. Once the stage is set, she will let go and have a wonderful time.

What Turns Virgo On—and Off

Earth sign Virgo enjoys a somewhat dubious reputation as inhibited. This is simply not true and equates discernment with prudishness. Virgo is a correct sign and is turned on by delicacy in manners and behavior. He is turned on by attention to details, and is very sensitive to a person's looks. Virgo is finicky about who touches him and wants sex to be rich and meaningful. Virgo men and women are wild about massage, herbs, good food, and natural scents. Both they and their partner must be clean. Whereas Taurus and Capricorn are earth signs that are lusty and don't mind a little mud and scent au naturel, Virgo delights in running from the bath to a bed with clean sheets and then beginning his tryst.

Once Virgo men or women are involved in a sexual relationship, they will still want lots of foreplay, wooing, and preliminaries. This sign usually has a very good imagination and can fantasize easily. Illustrated sex books or DVDs are definitely turn-ons. Because Virgo's imagination is so strong, a few suggestions will get him in the mood. Unlike the other earth signs, this sign likes to talk about sex. A conversation with the details of what he is going to do excites Virgo, even if it makes him blush. Then, when words become reality, Virgo has double the pleasure because he has already visualized a delicious encounter.

Written in the Stars

The single greatest Virgo turnoff is a sloppy or dirty partner. A relationship with such an individual just won't happen. Virgo will notice dirt under the fingernails, clothes that don't smell fresh, or hair that is a little greasy. And once she notices that, it's no sex for you two.

If a partner has passed the cleanliness test, another turnoff is a critical manner. Virgo has the challenge of being overly concerned with small details. She fights this tendency, but if her partner is critical even in a teasing way, then her mind will start working overtime, and her more sensual nature will freeze up. The time to talk about what you would like and what would feel good is before you start making love. If a Virgo starts giving or listening to instructions, she will lose her sexy focus and become inhibited.

Virgo's Strengths and Specialties

Virgo is a mutable sign because their birth month August–September begins in the summer and ushers us into the fall. Mutable signs are flexible; are hard-working; and can change their demands, desires, and needs according to circumstances.

Written in the Stars
Virgo looks young for her age and retains an innocence throughout her life. This quality enhances her sex appeal. It also means she can have relationships with partners of different ages. No one will even think about an age difference between the Virgo and her partner.

One of Virgo's great strengths in the bedroom is that he can accommodate anything that feels good and pleases both him and his partner. He might not be tremendously adventurous, but once sex is going well, he will not shrink from a new position or technique. He is not shy in describing his wants and desires before you begin, and will have a way of speaking about sex that is provocative and imaginative. If he describes something that will feel pleasurable, by the end of the description, you will both be eagerly anticipating the actual sexy event. Slow sensual rubbing and soothing are Virgo specialties.

Virgo's Weaknesses and Foibles

You already know about Virgo's desire for cleanliness, which can be a weakness. Also, be aware that if Virgo starts faultfinding, she can more quickly impede her own creativity and sensuality and that of her partner than any other sign. Virgo's mind works by making lists, and if she has lists of pleasures and special places on her and her partner's body that need and want kissing, her habit can be a treat in the bedroom. However, if the list becomes "this is good," "they didn't do that right," "this should be better," and "why didn't they do that," then Virgo will not enjoy anything, and no one will enjoy her.

The phrase "I fired him" to describe ending a relationship is something a Virgo might say. Such a cool and distant attitude will ensure that party time in the bedroom diminishes, and until Virgo lets go of that tendency, relationships of all kinds will suffer.

The Virgo Man

The Virgo man has a tendency to be a perfectionist. The way he demonstrates this is with exact planning of all the details that will ensure a good sexual encounter. He will pay attention to his own personal grooming, tidy up the house if his partner is coming over, cook, or choose a small, intimate restaurant and make sure it is not too far from home. Then as a sexy feeling builds, transportation worries will not threaten it. He sets the scene easily.

A little-known part of a Virgo man's sexual nature is that he is a very giving partner because he has few traditional hang-ups about sex. He likes the idea of learning about what pleases his partner, and is genuinely interested in what works and what doesn't. He is willing to admit when he doesn't know how to do something, but he is a quick study and happy to please once he knows what his partner desires. He will be content with all sexual positions, but may not be daring enough to initiate them. He will not enjoy anything involving messy or sticky food. The Virgo man does not like crumbs in the bed, and although massage is a turn-on, sliding all over the sheets is not Virgo's idea of sexy, passionate fun.

The Virgo Woman

Virgo women never advertise their sensuality. The symbol of the sign is a maiden with a sheaf of wheat, which symbolizes the harvest. Virgo's sensuality is as regular and fertile as the fruits of the earth, which are harvested every year. She has a highly developed sense of touch and smell. She will keep herself very put together and is usually fastidious about keeping her home. There are some sloppy, free-for-all Virgos, but even if there seems to be chaos in her home, she will have an internal sense of organization and can find whatever she needs. Virgo loves the dance of seduction, and anticipating the pleasure of a love affair is almost as good as the real encounter. When she gets to the bedroom, she enjoys white lingerie that is lacy and practical. Lingerie that is uncomfortable or overly decorated is not for the classic-loving Virgo. Gentle stroking of the hair, the back of the neck, and the temple area gives Virgo a feeling of ease and trust, and that translates into good lovemaking.

Setting the Scene

A Virgo would enjoy a country inn with a private hot tub. The partners can give each other massages with lavender-scented oil and then plunge into the hot tub to rub it all off. There are flip-flops and fluffy white terry cloth robes warmed from the sun or a heated towel rack. The bathroom may have a teak floor covering so that both you and Virgo can go from the bath to the bedroom without touching the naked floor. The details have been planned out beforehand, so there is nothing left to do but enjoy each other. Virgo doesn't care if it is day or night. He enjoys looking at his partner, whether in sunlight or candlelight. The scent of lemon verbena and a breeze gently blowing white curtains makes Virgo feel open, sexy, and ready.

Sexy Matches: The Hot and Not-So-Hot Combinations

If you are unhappy about one of the not-so-hot combos, keep in mind you may defy the odds. Don't analyze; see where life takes you.

Virgo and Aries

Virgo is not charmed by Aries's impetuosity, and that irritates Aries. Virgo is earth and Aries is fire, and although sometimes this combination of elements can mean a good short-term time in the bedroom, in this case, the planets ruled by Virgo and Aries are too contentious to light a spark. Virgo is ruled by Mercury, and Aries by Mars. Passion between these two signs is apt to be mentally stimulating but emotionally disconnected. If Virgo has a relationship with an Aries, they shouldn't expect constancy or interest in languid times in the bedroom. Breakneck speed and variety will typify this partner, and if those are not to Virgo's liking, it would be best for them to find another person.

Virgo and Taurus

These two earth signs flow together. A Taurus partner calms Virgo's mental activity, and since Virgo is usually a very good cook, Taurus is happy and eager to please Virgo. Taurus will not get involved with Virgo's list making and may just grab her, chuck the list, and steer them both toward more amusing and fruitful activity. It is a gift for Virgo to be able to feel first and think later.

When Stars Align

Virgo is known as the single-person sign. A short fling with good sex may be easier for Virgo than giving up his routine and forming a permanent relationship.

Virgo and Gemini

This combination is fun and possibly sexy, but not easy. Virgo and Gemini are both ruled by the planet Mercury. Virgo is earth and Gemini is air, and they are both mutable signs. They love communication, information, talking, all forms of oral stimulation, and anything that keeps them mentally engaged and not bored. In the bedroom, their different natures are apparent, as Virgo is firmly located in her body's sensuality and Gemini needs to concentrate to feel. Gemini is very active mentally, and is a great fantasizer and a great talker. Virgo likes this as a preliminary, but when you get right down to having sex, Virgo likes to feel sensual and not talk. A relationship between these two is always interesting. Both signs like to learn about sex and try out new things. They would enjoy going through a sex manual or online videos to experiment, but for a longer, committed relationship, unless Gemini has some earth in his chart, they may create dust.

Virgo and Cancer

The elements of earth and water are sexually compatible. Virgo and Cancer go well together, theoretically. Virgo likes the sincerity and sensitivity of a Cancerian. Virgo feels wanted and appreciated because Cancer is so ardent. On the other hand, the Cancerian may be shy about sex and slow to lead, and it is difficult for Virgo to initiate sex. If these two partners get together as friends first, then a sexual relationship is more likely.

Once in the bedroom, the moon child's sensitive skin and light touch is a turn-on for Virgo. Virgo must curb any tendency to criticize or rate Cancerian techniques or the success or failure of lovemaking. If he does not, Cancer will be out the door and never return.

> **Passion Points**
> Both Virgo and Cancer love to kiss and caress the belly.

Virgo and Leo

Mercury and the Sun, the respective ruling planets in this combination, make these two a fairly hot combo. These two can be physically very compatible even though their personalities are quite different. Virgo is content to be the backstage supporter for Leo's more dramatic personality and share her sensual nature with Leo's fiery temperament. Virgo needs a little zip in her life, as frequently she can become a slave to routine and lists of dos and don'ts. She is smitten with Leo because he always looks good, is generous, and pays absolutely no attention to the details that can inhibit Virgo. Long or short term, these two signs have a lot to share.

Virgo and Virgo

Earth and earth is a sexy combination. Partners between these two signs understand each other's sensual needs nonverbally. This ability helps both Virgos get into their bodies and out of their heads, and curtails the tendency to critique. Virgo is a sign of service, and this pair loves to switch roles in serving and being served, which can apply to oral sex as well as regular sex. They also enjoy a similar rhythm and are likely to be in the mood at the same time. Morning is probably the best time for Virgos to enjoy each other.

Virgo and Libra

Virgo and Libra are next-door-neighbor signs. Their elements, earth and air, are different, but sexual chemistry can work here because both signs believe discretion and good taste are very important. Virgo loves the romantic Libran, the care she takes in arranging dates, and the restaurants she chooses. Also, in the bedroom, there will be no extreme surprises between Virgo and Libra. Virgo's sensuality is good for Libra, who tends to get wrapped up in ideas about sex, plus Virgo's sensuality allows Libra to delight in the body.

Virgo and Scorpio

Although you may not think that Virgo can handle Scorpio's intensity, this combination can be hot because both signs are in compatible elements: earth and water. Virgo is not an extreme sign in terms of passion, but her rooted sensuality and ability to adapt makes her a sexy partner with a Scorpio. This is a fertile combination and good for a short-term or a committed relationship.

> **When Stars Align**
> For Scorpio, Virgo should use her virgin mystique. Virgo's purity appeals to Scorpio's intensity.

Virgo will have to ignore Scorpio's silent treatment when things are not going well. Scorpio tends to go underground to recoup, and Virgo will enjoy trying to perk Scorpio up, even if not successful. Oral pleasure is good between these two, as Scorpio loves all sensation, and the idea of being slightly wicked appeals to Virgo. One part of the attraction between the two signs is that a Virgo doesn't have to be a goody-goody and can play in the presence of Scorpio's passionate creativity.

Virgo and Sagittarius

There is attraction here, but controversy in rhythms. Sagittarians are ramblers, and their tendency to energetically pursue their own pleasures at their own tempo puts Virgo in a tizzy. A Sagittarian is alluring to a Virgo because of their differences. Virgo is attracted to Sag because Sagittarius is big-hearted and generous and almost entirely uninterested in the details that Virgo uses to order her world. Both signs are mutable; that is, they are able to change and adapt. When the Sagittarius's fire burns for Virgo, she will not resist because of the well-known Sagittarius charm. Sagittarius will keep Virgo laughing and never puts Virgo down for her fastidiousness. In the bedroom, Virgo will be appreciated by Sag. The thighs and legs are the areas to concentrate on. Sagittarius will definitely be the leader here.

Virgo and Capricorn

This is a serious combination, with a lot of comfort between the two people. Both are earth signs and very comfortable with sensuality. They have a highly tuned sense of touch. Both signs are very responsible and will not tend toward promiscuity. This is a combo for a long relationship rather than a short one because the two signs at first may come into conflict over the more negative aspects of each other's sexual personality: Capricorn worries and Virgo criticizes. If they can hit the sheets immediately and bypass these parts of their characters, the relationship will be launched and have room to grow.

Virgo and Aquarius

Astrologically speaking, the relationship between Virgo and Aquarius is called inconjunct, and this is a good way to describe the relationship between the two signs. They don't quite meet, but they interest each other because each is exotic to the other. Virgo says, "How can you be so unconventional? Don't you care what people think?" Aquarius says, "How can you be so conventional? Don't you like people thinking you are unique?" In the bedroom, these two attitudes can definitely be sexy, as both signs behave differently in private. A Virgo loves the idea of straightening up Aquarius, and Aquarius loves challenging Virgo's sense of orderliness. If both signs can play with each other, it will be a good short-term relationship. In a longer relationship, they might irritate each other too much.

Passion Points
Virgo rules the intestines, and so far, no one has succeeded in making that a particularly erogenous zone. For best results, try the back of the neck.

Virgo and Pisces

Opposite signs in compatible elements make for good times in bed, life, friendship, and long-term relationships. Dreamy Pisces complements Virgo's earthy sensuality because Pisces floats on feelings and is very capable of putting the world away and retreating into a world of sense and delight. Virgo loves to join this world because it renews and soothes. Tickling and giving hickeys in discreet places are great ways of beginning for Virgo and Pisces. If Virgo concentrates on Pisces's toes, they will embark on a beautiful voyage. Both signs love scented baths.

Sex Planets: Mars and Venus

To learn more about yourself and your partner, figure out in which sign his or her Venus and Mars are located. This information will add pizzazz to everything you have learned about your partner's Sun sign.

Mars in Virgo

Virgo's scope and interests are a little narrow for Mars's energy. Mars energy is fiery, and when in Virgo, it is difficult to corral that fire into the kind of organization and order that Virgo loves. Sex is inherently the province of Mars, so when a person has this signature or if your partner has this position, you know right away that lovemaking cannot be random or without care for details. There will be lots of sexy verbal description and energy in the way Mars in Virgo speaks.

Usually Virgo with this placement enjoys sensuality almost more than sex itself. He is not shy, but the beauty of a shoulder or a delicately shaped earlobe catches him up, and he pauses to caress this part of his partner's body. If you want to please your Mars in Virgo partner, make sure everything runs smoothly and that there are no bumps or sudden surprises. Mars in Virgo can get offtrack easily.

Venus in Virgo

Venus is not considered well placed in Virgo. The easy, pleasure-loving nature of Venus goes against the grain of fastidious, organized Virgo. In the bedroom, Venus in Virgo needs to remember one maxim: feel first, think later. Start with a massage and avoid any lengthy discussions of who is going to do what and how. The body responds to touch, and the scent of orange water or lemon blossom will help things develop. A lightly scented spray discreetly applied would be something that makes Venus in Virgo feel sexy. There is a formal feeling to Venus in Virgo. She enjoys dressing well in the muted colors of blue, white, black, and ivory, but her undergarments will rarely be black. If you are pursuing a person with this placement, emphasize rhythmic and steady physical contact. Kisses that are moist and not too wet will be most successful.

Chapter 7

Libra

(September 23–October 22)

Libra, the seventh sign of the zodiac, is the only sign whose symbol, the Scales, is an inanimate object. The need to balance and examine gives Librans a detached quality that sometimes makes them seem less than warm and cuddly. However, in one-on-one sexual relations, Libra has one of the most attractive, sexy energies of the zodiac. Venus, or Aphrodite for the ancient Greeks, is the goddess of love, and Libra, ruled by Venus, is a devoted acolyte to romantic love, sexual love, friendly love, and marital love.

The Romantic

Libra often goes from one extreme to the other before coming to a decision. Making decisions about anything is a challenge, but in the process, he will weigh all sides of the argument. It is the sign of partnership, and a Libra likes to be in a partnership to discover his own needs and wants. As Libra matures, he will find the balance within himself and have more inner reserves to share. Until that time, there will be lots of sexual drama in relationships.

Libra has a refined nature, and she responds to all romantic gestures. She likes flowers, sweet words, and little gifts, and needs to feel wanted. It is easy to get physical with her when she believes that there is romantic potential in the relationship. She can see the romantic hero or heroine in front of her, even if they are wearing sweatpants and a T-shirt. The important thing for Libra is the expectation that sex will lead to relationship harmony. Once this romantic idea surfaces with Libra, she will pursue or allow herself to be pursued and will be the most pleasant partner imaginable.

Written in the Stars

Saving little sentimental presents, like the sugar cubes from the restaurant where you first met, is an excellent way to move Libra from simply thinking about a physical relationship with you to actually engaging in one.

In the physical department, she will be reserved, but can also satisfy your more creative sexual fantasies because you are the subject of her romantic dream. Libras like to marry and may marry often, but whether they plan to marry you or not, they need the illusion that this is more than a one-night stand. Her physical fires burn within the expectation of forever.

The charming aspect of Libra's romanticism in terms of sex is that he is ardent and passionate and always sees the best in his partner. He will work hard to please his mate. The flush of love gives him permission to be as sexy and wild as he likes. Then, when the next fling comes along, he will say that he had it all wrong, and that this is the one.

What Turns Libra On—and Off

Libra is turned on by being out in social occasions with her special date. While she is socializing with others, the tingle of knowing what comes afterward when she and her mate are alone is tremendously exciting. The refined nature of Libra's mind sometimes gives her a snobby opinion of other people. She requires a very put-together look that fits in with the occasion, and does not like anything too dramatic or ostentatious. Innately, a Libran knows good clothes and wants her partner to wear them.

Libra rules the kidneys, which are not noteworthy for inspiring sexy feelings. But the area of the lower back is sensitive. Massage this area, and if you stroke or put slight pressure on this area when in the midst of making love, it will be especially satisfying.

When Libra's romantic idea machine is activated, he responds passionately to his partner, but there is little that is truly wild and abandoned with Libra in the sex department. He has a strong sex drive but is not unpredictable. He can mirror the way you'd like it and is happy to please, but his turn-ons are conventional: kissing, cuddling, engaging in two or three tried-and-true positions, and, if you spend the night, spooning. This repertoire is never boring, because there is such delight and charm being with Libra that you feel satisfied even if you have a penchant for more experimental sex. A rhythm in lovemaking that is steady is also a turn-on for Libra. At the grand finale, he can be very vocal, but never loud enough to wake up neighbors.

The major turnoff for Libra is not feeling wanted. She has difficulty overcoming a feeling of rejection if, for any reason, her partner is not in the mood. She can pout and cajole and be charming, but may become whiny when she doesn't get what she wants. If her partner isn't keen too many times when she is, then that's the end of the relationship.

Also, Libra is not keen on dirty talk or crude language. Talking about sex and bodily functions is a turnoff. Librans, whatever they do in the bedroom, like to be ladies and gentlemen.

Libra's Strengths and Specialties

This sign above all others is interested in pleasing his partner. He will push himself to explore wilder sex than he might initiate if it will delight his partner. He also is an equal-orgasm partner and will do everything possible to get the timing right so no one feels cheated. Two great strengths for a Libra are his beauty and charm. He will take care of himself, wear clothes that suit him perfectly, and compliment and appreciate the way his partner looks. Libra is strongest when he is in a partnership. Intimate relations for Libra are part of an aesthetic and physical desire. Not only should making love feel good, but it should be beautiful; it shouldn't include scratchy garments, harsh lighting, tawdry rooms, or impromptu hidden corners.

> **Written in the Stars**
> Heavy perfume or cologne are major turnoffs for Libra.

Once you have the surroundings, foreplay does not have to be touching, kissing, or oral sex. The best way to get a Libra hot is to invent a romantic date for the two of you in an elegant atmosphere. It doesn't have to be expensive, just romantic, but a fast-food joint will not cut it. A little-known tip about Libra's sexual desires is that she enjoys physical sensation on both sides of the body. A kiss on the left side means a kiss on the right side should be next. This will add a certain je ne sais quoi to your date and encourage a repeat.

Libra's Weaknesses and Foibles

Physically, Libra is not robust. In the boudoir, this means that all-night sex marathons are a rare occasion. Libra heats up just fine, but after "making the beast with two backs," as Shakespeare put it, Libra is ready for a deep sleep. He is also not wild about highly adventurous sexual practices or positions. Bondage and discipline hold little appeal. A Libran may enjoy being dominant, but the accoutrements of whips and leather are too extreme for his sense of good taste. If you want to use a set of silken ropes that glide easily over the skin, Libra might give this a try.

Like her fellow air signs, Gemini and Aquarius, Libra has a touch of claustrophobia and will not be sexually responsive in any way if she is in an environment that is narrow, dark, and stuffy. Doing it in caves, tunnels, or even parked cars on a secluded lane could produce a panic attack.

Lastly, it must be said that Libra can be a merciless flirt and delights in attracting a partner and not following through.

The Libra Man

As Libra symbolizes the desire to balance opposites, you may expect a Libra man to be highly attuned to his feminine side. He has a refined sense of taste and beauty and will want his partner to be stylish, gentle, and well-mannered in public. In the bedroom, the manners won't be necessary. Being friendly with his own feminine side makes a Libra man a terrific partner who is able to intuit exactly what will please his love. And his charming smile will more than likely ensure that he, in turn, receives what he needs and desires. It's all a question of balance with Libra, and as the zodiac's most partnership-oriented sign, the Libra man knows the give-and-take of sex without even trying.

A Libra man will not enjoy watching sexy videos of other people, but he may be enough of an exhibitionist to make one for himself. If he feels confident in his and his partner's looks, it could be a sexy night while the cameras are rolling.

As an air sign, he may be more tuned into the mental idea of sex rather than physical lust. He will put his partners on a pedestal and, when imagining them as a work of art, could be shocked when he realizes that they are flesh and blood and not a perfect statue. Getting down to it physically may take a little time, and the Libra man can be thrown by little bumps. For example, if the phone rings in the middle of things, it will take him a while to get back on course. But he will re-engage and keep going to a good conclusion.

Passion Points

The left side of the hip leading down to the thigh is a place most Libran men find highly stimulating. You can start by caressing that sweet spot and move right on down from there.

The Libra Woman

Venus, goddess of beauty and love, is Libra's ruler, and don't ever forget it. The Libra woman loves everything to do with pursuing, keeping, renewing, and revitalizing a one-on-one relationship. She may be better at a relationship with a partner and have real problems staying "just friends" if the nature of her or your desire changes. This woman is also a terrible flirt. Her smile is so charming and lights up her entire face. This is genuine and makes people on the street happy that she has greeted them. In more intimate surroundings, the Libra woman demands lots of romance, lots of attention to seductive details such as mood music, flowers, scent, and beautiful bed linens. Her fiddling with the atmosphere might make a lustier sign impatient. She'll enjoy sex if you enjoy sex, but may be a little shy about discussing it. As the queen, she somehow expects the king to know exactly what she would like. If this slightly old-fashioned scenario is not producing results, Libra will find a very cute and nonconfrontational way to say, "Darling, why don't you try this?" Then you both will be content.

Libra women have a masculine side, and can be very assertive out of the bedroom. The sign is frequently described as the steel hand in a velvet glove. She is so tactful and mindful of another's feelings that before you know what hit you, you are in the romantic idyll that Libra needs as a prelude for more intimate contact. She will be a fabulous ear nuzzler, loves to caress your neck, and worships the fact that you take the time to keep your body fit. It all redounds to her credit because she is in love with love, and for this moment, that love is you.

Setting the Scene

The evening is slightly warm, the moon halfway to full, and Venus, the evening star, is twinkling on the horizon. Your dinner with flowers and candlelight was effervescent. You both look good, and now, as you stroll to your rendezvous, something stronger than a goodnight kiss is on your mind. Libra isn't fussy about where to get physical as long as the room is beautiful, clean, and private. If she is traveling to your place, expect silk underwear to pop out of her bag just to get things off to an aesthetically pleasing start. In her home, she might place lavender scent on the sheets and have diaphanous curtains on the windows to let in the moonlight.

Scented candles glow. A chaise lounge is opposite the bed, and you lounge there for a time, with lots of kisses all over the neck and arms. Because the whole evening has been so delicious, you and your Libra partner are perfectly in sync. There isn't much talk except for sweet murmurs, and then, at some point, she leads you from the chaise to the bed. With eyes open and dazzling, you have beautiful, delicious, and tender sex. Libra the Prince or Libra the Princess feels balanced and complete because, for that moment, it's love.

Sexy Matches: The Hot and Not-So-Hot Combinations

Libra, the sign of relationships, is passionately interested in having the right partner where there is a possibility for a long-term run. Sometimes this is a Libran delusion, as that particular guy or girl is only a fling, but somehow the Libra still imagines that each fling could last forever. When you read these combinations, use your mind to understand that a not-so-hot combo may be irresistible and a delightful experience. Go ahead and see what happens; Libra is not famous for self-discipline.

Libra and Aries

The opposite signs in air and fire, respectively, attract each other and have a tempestuous relationship. A *bonfire* may be a better word. Aries is the "me first" sign, and Libra, the "after you" sign. This conflict is hot in the bedroom but is wearing on the nerves for the long term. Aries emphasizes straight physical contact while Libra provides the romantic touches. She will have to do it because Aries is usually too much in a hurry. The best part of this combination is that it is laughter filled. Where there are jokes and giggles, good sex is not far away.

Libra and Taurus

Venus is the ruler of both these signs, but their elements are different: air and earth. This is a steady, sensual, languid, solid, hot duo. The connection is good for a flirt or a long-term partnership. Libra thrills to Taurus's romantic side. The Libra may be impatient with Taurus's pace, which is a bit slower than Libra's, but the physical relationship works because both signs share similar sensibilities. They are calmed by eating sweets, and sharing these in bed will lead to other pleasures. Oral sex is a good place to start for both signs, but the main course is the chief attraction.

Libra and Gemini

A relationship between this airy combination could not be more fun. Both signs are mentally oriented, so their particular brand of sexual pleasure should be called exciting, rather than lusty. Libra will enjoy Gemini's try-anything approach and take a peek at activities lacking in her own sexual repertoire. The speed with which Gemini changes his mind frustrates Libra. Libra has a hard-enough time making a decision, so when Gemini in the sack starts one way, then goes another, Libra may be a beat behind. The positive aspect of this duo is that they will be able to communicate about their desires and come to a satisfying compromise.

Libra and Cancer

Venus and the Moon are the ruling planets, and the elements are air and water, in this hot and inspired combo. Traditionally, this combo is called a square astrological relationship and is not known for ease.

However, both signs are so tuned in to picking up other people's vibes that when they are on the same frequency they create a beautiful bubble of sexual contentment. Libra loves pleasing Cancer because Libra delights in creating a homey atmosphere that makes Cancer feel comfortable and passionate. Cancer is a sign that understands and is sentimental about dating rituals, and Libra laps this up. Cancer's emotional moodiness can be too much for Libra sometimes as Libra tries to balance Cancer's tidal waves of feeling, but if Libra doesn't think too much, Libra can have a very good time. Kissing the chest and tummy are turn-ons for this duo.

Libra and Leo

What an opportunity for this air and fire combo! Both signs like to socialize and to show off in public. Looking good and receiving confirmation that you look good is a prime aphrodisiac for L and L. Exhibitionistic sex is usually not an option with Libra, so Leo's more daring temperament will have to be satisfied with a private showing at home or a more secluded place, but there is ample room for fun and games here. Choose daylight dates, perhaps around three in the afternoon, and Leo and Libra will both be happy. Libra likes the assertive side of Leo. If Leo forgets to roar and becomes a kitten instead, Libra may pass on future dates.

> **Passion Points**
> Both Libra and Leo are sensitive in the lower back.
> Caress the hollow, and the sexual engines will start
> roaring.

Libra and Virgo

This air and earth combination can be too fussy to have a good time between the sheets. Libra flits around, trying to get the right romantic mood, and Virgo obsesses about striving for perfection. There's too much planning and not enough sensual touching. The signs are next-door neighbors but may not get to spark each other physically. There is appreciation and admiration but not enough creative tension to make a hot combo.

Libra and Libra

The duo of these romantic signs is a delight for everyone around them. Between themselves, they enjoy each other's company, know how to please the other, and are a good couple. This couple will decide "Okay, let's go to bed together," have a great time, and then wonder if they made the right decision. But they will be happy to make the same decision again and again. The sheer beauty of both partners will delight them for a long time. Parting could be the most difficult decision they make, so they may stay together just so no one's feelings get hurt.

Libra and Scorpio

This can be a sexy combination, but slightly off balance for Libra. Libra's ruler is Venus, and Scorpio's ruler in ancient astrology was Mars. Their differences are evident in that Venus and Mars delineate the primal male and female polarity. Libra fears to dive into Scorpio's deep waters and can be turned off by her intensity. Libra is not strong enough to take Scorpio's emotional zingers and does not take pleasure in the Scorpion's sting. For a short trip through a darker world than Libra usually inhabits, this could be a hot combo, but it doesn't satisfy either sign or last long.

Libra and Sagittarius

Venus and Jupiter are the ruling planets here, and the sheer lucky and exuberant nature of both signs makes this a buoyant and hot tryst. Libra loves the full-frontal approach that Sag is known for. Libra laughs when Sag is clumsy, even in bed, because Sag laughs too. This is a fun affair but has one drawback: the famous Sagittarian frankness is too much for Libra. Libra doesn't want a candid opinion on anything. If these two want to enjoy themselves, they must declare a moratorium on conversing in bed. Cooing, humming, and keeping their mouths filled with various body parts will be much more successful than talking.

Libra and Capricorn

Both signs are cardinal leadership signs, but are in inharmonious elements, air and earth. The combination is too serious to satisfy either sign. Libra likes varied, mental, light connections, and Capricorn likes lusty, sensual ones. They cramp each other's styles, and in the bedroom, there is too much effort for too little pleasure. Libra does enjoy Capricorn's good taste and solidity, plus his bank account may be a turn-on, but for physical satisfaction, these two might need to look elsewhere.

Libra and Aquarius

These are both air signs with exciting ruling planets: Venus and Uranus. Even though the elements are compatible, Libra cannot accept Aquarian eccentricity and abruptness. She also does not participate in the all-friends-invited Aquarian idea of sexual freedom. These two communicate well but exist in different universes. Sexually, if the Aquarian dominates a Libran, and the two people are cool with this relationship, then these air signs may have a compatible, airy sexual relationship.

When Stars Align

A gift between Libra and Aquarians could be anything with a rainbow motif. Both signs love the colors of the rainbow. Libra, if you are pursuing an Aquarius, throw in some conversation about the colors of each chakra, and your seduction is accomplished.

Libra and Pisces

Venus and Neptune are probably one of the dreamiest combinations of the zodiac. Sex between them is not hot and spicy; it is more lukewarm and sweet, like warm pudding. Pisces is tender and refined, and Libra always responds well to a delicate touch. However, remember that Libra women have some masculine qualities, and vice versa for the men. Libra and Pisces satisfy only one part of Libra's nature. They can escape together into a hazy, happy world, but Libra doesn't want to stay there too long: it could be bad for the complexion and waistline. After a few dates, Pisces's phlegmatic nature and Libra's indecision can wear on these two.

Sex Planets: Mars and Venus

To get the full scoop on sexual chemistry, find out the Mars and Venus placements for you and your partner. Considering these as well as the Sun sign will increase your understanding of a partner's and your own libido.

Mars in Libra

Warlike Mars in Libra's sign is not considered well placed because the assertive thrust of Mars can't be expressed with all that back-and-forth and balancing that Libra is prone to. The person with this placement may have real problems making a decision and finds sex a challenge because at first, one thing looks good, and then you could also do that position, or try this other one. The desire to please may attract a more definite partner who can harness Mars in Libra's libido and focus it. There is a refined quality with this placement, and a partner with this position is extremely fair and legally oriented. He tends to speak as if he were cross-examining someone, which is perhaps not the best sort of dialogue between the sheets. Tasteful and friendly books about sex are good for this placement to consider because it will get the fantasy wheels in motion and help give him some ideas about what to do. Teasing and tickling are great preliminaries, as is biting. Love bites are one way that Mars in Libra can satisfy his need for aggression but still maintain a cute quotient. Mars in Libra may also be very subtle about seduction. While he has the intention of going to bed, this placement does not want to make a move that appears crude or vulgar. Don't miss that extra pressure on the small of his back as you dance. It can be filled with meaning.

Venus in Libra

This position is the love goddess personified. Venus is Libra's ruler, and when she is placed here, a person is incredibly romantic and idealistic in love. She may also be naive about the qualities of her partner, for she sees the one she loves through rose-colored glasses. There is nothing quite like the delight of having one of these charming partners. She will prepare your favorite foods, dress to please, be a stimulating conversationalist, and, in bed, elevate lovemaking to worshipful harmony.

Lust is not her strong point, but you may not even notice because what she does offer is so delightful. If you like to get down and have sex in public or in hidden corners, or in any extreme way, this is not the lass for you. With Venus in Libra, the ideas of romance, sex, and partnership all blend together to create a truly beautiful experience. Orgasms may bring her to tears, and she is supportive and encouraging to her partner.

Chapter 8

Scorpio
(October 23–November 21)

Scorpio, one of the powerhouse fixed signs,
is the strongest sign of the zodiac. It is
the eighth sign and the second water sign.
Unsurprisingly, Mars was Scorpio's ruler
until Pluto was discovered in 1930. Scorpio
is a yin (feminine) sign, and the power of
this sign is attractive and magnetic rather
than outgoing and assertive. You will sense
Scorpio's presence and may feel inexplicably
drawn to him, but you should hesitate.
His sexuality is complex, and casual ease
is not his strong point.

The Extremist

Scorpio's strength is the passionate creativity and intensity with which she approaches everything, including and especially sex. The question for every Scorpio is whether she will emphasize creation or destruction. Scorpio has three symbols: the scorpion, the eagle, and the phoenix. The scorpion would rather sting herself to death than forego the pleasure of the sting. This symbol represents the unevolved Scorpio, who is frequently trapped in a cycle of pleasurable hedonism that can lead to excess. The next symbol is the eagle, which represents the spirit soaring toward the sun, but which also is a fierce hunter. The final and most evolved symbol for Scorpio is the phoenix, a bird that destroys itself and then rises again from its ashes. When an evolved Scorpio masters the ability to turn the dark aspects of her character into light, all her power is creative. The effects can be spectacular and healing.

Passion Points

You guessed it! The genitals and tush are ruled by Scorpio, and that means by definition the sexiest and most pleasurable parts of the body are part of his dominion. Kissing, sucking, squeezing, massaging, spanking, poking, and goosing these areas are all parts of Scorpio's lovemaking arsenal.

Wherever Scorpio is in his personal development, he is sexually hot. Scorpio is known as the sex sign because of the power that the sign contains. After all, what is sex but sharing energy in a focused, intense way? Scorpio is at the forefront of the battle of the bedroom. As partners, Scorpios are willing to explore the heights and depths of sexual expression. Partners beware—but don't miss the experience.

It is possible for Scorpio to be celibate! That might sound like a shocking statement, but if she decides to curtail her sexual energy, she is quite capable of doing so. It may not be the easiest choice, but Scorpio will hew to it and believe it to be productive for her life. Extremes for Scorpio mean all sorts of things. Perhaps the most well-known Scorpio who considered the issue of celibacy was St. Augustine, who was a pagan and then adopted Christianity. After a profligate and lusty youth, St. Augustine prayed, "Lord, make me chaste, but not yet." This is not a common path, but it speaks to the Scorpio who doesn't want to share his sexual power. Such Scorpios are still powerful and intense.

Extreme sexual behaviors for Scorpio usually have some element of dominance and submission scenarios. Scorpio likes power but attracts it in a subtle, almost hypnotic fashion. You want to look; you thrill to look; you are nervous to look; but you do look, and the experience is fascinating. For Scorpio, sex is not casual, it is bigger than that.

The feeling of possessing or being possessed is a major part of Scorpio's extremism. This sign doesn't fool around with flirtation, dating rituals, kisses, or polite sex. A fling is not casual, but instead an experience in lust that awakens every part of the body.

What Turns Scorpio On—and Off

Turn-ons center on snaring a receptive partner in Scorpio's web. If he looks at you with lust and you involuntarily blush, that is a victory for Scorpio and means things can advance. Scorpio acts with confidence in sexual matters. He likes to affect people and undress them with his eyes, knowing that with a particular look or well-chosen word, a fantasy will become reality.

Written in the Stars

A sexy voice is one of the Scorpion's best seduction tools. It shimmers with innuendo and passion. Whispers during sex, phone sex before you get together, or outrageously funny sex talk are all areas of expertise for Scorpio.

Scorpio is turned on by let-it-all-hang-out sexiness in a person's dress and fashion. A tight pair of pants with gold embellishments is not too extreme. Her motto is "If you've got it, flaunt it," and she is not particularly concerned with good taste. Scorpio does enjoy high fashion and is especially fond of fashions that are revealing and exhibit her best features. Fashion also reveals status in life, and Scorpio likes to exhibit her accomplishments.

Engaging in different sexual positions, enjoying oral sex, using whips and chains, or being tied to a chair are all expressions of sexuality that are turn-ons for Scorpio. His motivation is neither pleasure nor pain but the power that is unleashed between two people when there is a fearsome intimacy. This kind of hot sexual connection can foster lifelong bonds of love and friendship, but such sexual expression doesn't usually come casually. Although Scorpio's appetites may lead him to a one-night stand, his deepest pleasure is exploring sexual life with a consistent partner. Ultimately, Scorpio is turned on by the trust that wild sex can foster. Two partners who feel this trust share the secret of their sex life, and that is a powerful and sexy bond.

Other turn-ons are wordless understandings that you are going to have sex. At a party, if you and he are already partners, and he gives you a nod and you disappear into a parked car, the thrill of the sex is multiplied by the implicit possession that the nod conveys.

Lust for Scorpio is always emotional. He cannot disconnect from his passions and feelings. His partners can respond with any kind of feeling, and it won't throw Scorpio. In fact, he delights in emotionality because that gives heat to desire and intimacy.

Turnoffs for Scorpio are cool characters that are nonresponsive to Scorpio's games. If Scorpio wanted, she could probably nuke them in the sensual department, but why waste time on a block of ice? Equally unappealing to Scorpio is superficiality. Scorpios are not silly people, and the intensity with which they pursue life must at least be appreciated, if not mirrored, by partners. Scorpio equates superficiality with easy conquest, and then there is not much interest or excitement.

Lacking a sense of humor also turns off Scorpio. The Scorpio usually has a wicked sense of humor. His remarks about other people can be stinging but painfully funny. Scorpio is not shackled by the polite convention of saying only nice things. When Scorpio and his partner laugh together at the human comedy, it creates an intimacy between them that makes both people feel connected and special. Then the world is a private joke, and sexual success, their private joy.

Scorpio's Strengths and Specialties

Sex is Scorpio's strength and specialty. In terms of sexual expression, Scorpio has the most staying power of all the water signs. She does not need to sleep and can happily retire to a dungeon or beautiful bedroom for extended sexual games. Consider Scorpio the Olympic athlete of sex.

She is also a master of the mysterious and will never tell what goes on behind closed doors. If you and Scorpio work together, consider the affair safe from anyone else in the office. Part of the pleasure for her will be the concealment.

If you have a particular penchant for some sexual whim you heard about once, then Scorpio is the partner for you. She delights in giving pleasure when someone reveals a secret lust. This also ensures that if she is interested in keeping you, she knows your secret. This knowledge can be fodder for the manipulation at which Scorpio is a master. She will make no secret about her ability to manipulate; just watch her get what she wants even if you think you have a better idea.

> **Written in the Stars**
> You do not need to compliment Scorpio about sexual equipment. They have a very good idea of how they rate. Scorpio hates idle flattery.

Needless to say, with Scorpio's sexual confidence, you can expect expertise in the boudoir. He will intuit what you want and may give it to you or may not. This is part of the delicious tease and power struggle that constitutes sexual relations for Scorpio. If this sounds risky, it is. But Scorpios have never shied away from risk, and in fact adore the thrill and spice it brings to life.

Scorpio's Weaknesses and Foibles

Scorpio's privacy mania can get too intense for a partner's comfort. It is a jealous sign and wants to control his partner until he is through with them. A simple date should not require a security check. And then, as the relationship progresses, Scorpio indulges in cross-examination if you are slightly late, or if he catches you with a mutual friend out of the corner of his eye. You say, "We were just walking to the coffee shop." Scorpio says, "Don't give me that. I know you want him." A Cancer will sulk when he believes a partner has been unfaithful. A Pisces will snivel and say, "Oh, well." But a Scorpio will decide you are either in or out. If you are out, that is it.

Written in the Stars

No matter how evolved a Scorpio may be, when wounded, he does not swallow the insult. Vengeance is the preferred method of handling insults, betrayal, and double-crossing. Scorpio doesn't hire a hit man or fill your glass with poison, but you will feel the sting of his revenge if you cross this secretive, powerful sign.

If for any reason a Scorpio has repressed her natural power, her weaknesses can be spectacularly self-destructive. Her needs will dominate, and her complaints will ooze throughout her circle of acquaintances and make everyone feel miserable. This is the draining, gloomy Scorpio, and it is almost impossible to get her out of her bad mood until she wills it.

Scorpio's self-control is very strong, and because he is so highly sexed, he may become overly self-involved with his prowess and forget that sex requires two to tango. Scorpio can be very self-centered and leave his partner outside his circle of pleasure. In such a situation, he may get off on servicing you or being serviced, but will never really connect.

The Scorpio Man

Quiet, alert, poised for danger, and informed about everything, a Scorpio man is a formidable competitor in life's games and in the bedroom. These guys are frequently artists, psychiatrists, detectives, researchers, and devotees of anything that seems profound, mysterious, and sexy. Whatever they do in life, they will know their subject thoroughly and carry a whiff of black magic about them. This man is not a gregarious social butterfly. Parties are opportunities to case the joint for future dates who want to experience profound pleasure and intimacy.

The Scorpio man is usually multitalented. If he is in business, he probably also has an artistic hobby such as playing music or doing magic. If he is an artist, he may very well also study finance and be a whiz at investing in the stock market. Whatever the Scorpio man appears to be is not the whole truth. He has layers and layers of intricate abilities and desires.

> **Written in the Stars**
> All the water signs are very sexy, but their motivations are totally different. Cancer wants to feel emotionally connected, Pisces wants to feel a hot escape from the everyday world, and Scorpio wants to indulge in the deepest secrets of physical intimacy. The result in each case is hot sex, but how you get there makes life interesting.

Most interesting about a Scorpio is that they know about lust but are more interested in a consistent relationship. All the outrageous possibilities that are in Scorpio's nature take root when there is a love that has a future. He may still question like the Grand Inquisitor, lock his partner in with him for a weekend of delight, and survey the field for other sweeties, but in the end, a Scorpio needs someone with whom he can share his profound experiences. Are you surprised? He also makes a loyal, considerate mate and a fierce protector of the family.

The Scorpio Woman

The spy Mata Hari had nothing on the mysterious, charming, and sexy Scorpio woman. A Scorpio woman can't be called a lady unless it is her role of the moment. She can act the part, but the Scorpio woman is too much ruled by her passions to fit such a tame label. Mars is usually associated with the fiery element, but in Scorpio, whose element is water, the Mars energy steams. She heats up the whole system with an intoxicating mix of determination, lust, and unknown pleasures. She is a bit kinky. If her partner doesn't want to go that route, she will oblige, but sooner or later, her intense desires have to be satisfied.

The Scorpio woman's power is not limited to the bedroom. She achieves in whatever area that she chooses. In business, she is a tough competitor; as a mother, she is devoted to her family; and if she is an artist, her creations will reflect her profound understanding of the mysteries of life.

Sex for her is power, but so are money, knowledge, mastery, and psychological insights. She doesn't fall in love; she allows herself to mingle with a partner, and reveals herself slowly. Life between the sheets is part of this striptease, not only of the body but also of the soul. The Scorpio woman is intense, and there is no use pretending that a relationship with her will be a fling or a one-night stand—unless she wants it that way. She can be totally caught up in a relationship and then decide it isn't for her. She will be honorable in telling her partner, but that's the way it will be, and she can't or won't do anything about it.

There are two roads to a Scorpio woman's heart: sex and secrets. If the first goes well, then she will share her secrets with you, which is a step forward in your relationship. If the sex is not working, there will be no secrets and no relationship. This will be fairly clear within one or two dates.

Setting the Scene

You and your Scorpio will take a trip through the jungle or through the depths of a swamp. Wild alligators, a few snakes, and the consistent hum of the birds calling are all part of this safari. There is an inn in this steamy paradise, and each room has a veranda that looks out into the savage vegetation. You and Scorpio check in for a week. The drums from a neighboring tribe beat a welcome for all the guests. You and your Scorpio drink martinis in the bar and then go up to your room. It is simple, with a large white wicker bed. Off come the safari clothes, and you both dive under the mosquito netting and get to it. Your sighs, groans, and screams fit in with the vibrating sounds of the jungle.

Written in the Stars

Garnets are one of the stones associated with Scorpio. Although you can't necessarily woo a Scorpio with gifts unless she wants to be wooed, garnets are a good choice. The blood-red color reminds Scorpios of the mysteries of life that interest them and usually complements their complexions.

Or, closer to home and with fewer bugs: you are giving a speech in front of a lot of colleagues, and your Scorpio partner stands next to you waiting for his turn to speak. You are both respected and known in your professions. Right after you finish, he whispers in your ear, "Let's go to my place. You look hot and I feel titanic." You sit down with a blush and giggle, and the first part of the Scorpio seduction is accomplished. When you arrive at his place, there is a race to the bedroom, but before you get there, you have a quickie standing against the kitchen counter. Relaxing in the huge bed, Scorpio brings out two dark red robes, and you lounge, drinking brandy. A bit later on, after sitting on a fur rug in front of the fire and eating smoked oysters, you settle into an easy and slow sexual rhythm. Wherever and whenever you mingle with Scorpio, you feel possessed by a hypnotizing love potion that keeps you enthralled.

Sexy Matches: The Hot and Not-So-Hot Combinations

If Scorpio so chooses, any zodiacal combination can be hot. It is his willpower that decides the future of a relationship, and he delights in proving astrology and astrologers incorrect. For Scorpio, there are some combos that are more challenging and interesting than others; let Scorpio choose which.

Scorpio and Aries

The ruling planets of Mars and Mars, with the elements of water and fire, create a boiling cauldron of sexual potency. The inherent competition in both signs makes this combo hot and worth the effort for both partners. They enjoy one-upmanship and are a match in terms of energy. Scorpio is the more intense, and over time, her love of mystery and covert activity will tire Aries, who is more of the moment and impetuous. Before exasperation sets in, these two are definitely sexual forces to reckon with.

Scorpio and Taurus

Opposite powerhouse signs in water and earth definitely attract. This is a hot combo for the short or long term. Once they fuse in a sexual and romantic relationship, it is very difficult for them to part. Taurus's earth soothes and stabilizes Scorpio's more destructive tendencies, but they meet in terms of loyalty and steady, sexy power. The sexual kick here is that Scorpio believes herself to be stronger than Taurus, and Taurus believes himself to be stronger than Scorpio—but both are good at keeping secrets, so neither feels let down.

Scorpio and Gemini

This is potentially an intriguing combo, but is not a hot one. Scorpio is the most intensely focused sign, and Gemini is the most scattered sign. Scorpio sexuality is all about the depths of life and passion, and Gemini flits around sexual ideas because they entertain the mind. Scorpio's staying power and willingness to initiate anything will find a willing mate in Gemini, but they are like the experience of eating a food that fills you up but doesn't satisfy. They will enjoy each other once or twice, but their elements, water and air, do not blend. Scorpio will usually feel Gemini is not worth the riches of his profound feelings.

> ### When Stars Align
> Scorpio is an under-wraps sign. He cherishes his privacy and will not reveal anything that he doesn't want other people to know. He can be passionate, but giving his heart is a different experience and takes longer. His real feelings are always very covert.

Scorpio and Cancer

Water and water are the elements here in the astrologically harmonious relationship called a trine. The ruling planets, Pluto and the Moon, mean that a sexual combination between these signs is hot and not casual. Scorpio may initiate Cancer into some of the more exotic parts of Cancerian's nature, and Cancer will enjoy the emotional closeness and feeling that they can have together. This is a relationship for the long and short term. It is fertile for building a family (if they choose) or other creative endeavors.

Scorpio and Leo

These are powerhouse signs in the elements of water and fire. Both these signs are sexual superstars in their own sphere, and when they come together, the Pluto rule of Scorpio and the Sun of Leo create formidable sex. Scorpio's predatory tendency to look for the vulnerable spots in her mate will, however, mark the end of the relationship. It is difficult for Leo's pride to withstand Scorpio's scrutiny. Scorpio intrinsically likes to take off the masks people wear, and Leo has no intention of discarding the mask. Let the good times roll for as long as they can.

☀ When Stars Align

In times of trouble, Scorpio is the most loyal sign of the zodiac. She understands the depths and heights of human experience, and if you need a friend in tough times and have been her friend, you can rely on her.

Scorpio and Virgo

Water and earth are hot here. As you can probably intuit, there is no contest in the intensity department between these two signs. Scorpio is the leader, and Virgo a good partner. Virgo's earthy sensuality feeds Scorpio, and for that reason, even though Virgo may not ever be as daring, extreme, or highly sexed as Scorpio, the combo of the two is good. Secretly, Scorpio believes that some of his more murky feelings may be redeemed by Virgo's purity. Remember, Scorpio, in every aspect of his life, seeks transformation.

Scorpio and Libra

Scorpio's ancient ruler is Mars, and, of course, Libra's ruler is Venus. There is excitement between these two signs, and between the sheets, they can have a fairly hot time. Quarreling is a definite spur to lovemaking, and Libra may lose the war but often wins the battles. Scorpio's love of mystery is unfathomable to Libra. These two may not last, but the experience will be hot for the duration.

Scorpio and Scorpio

This is a frequent, harmonious, and hot combination. It is fascinating to both partners as they see who will win which encounter. These master manipulators are unable to manipulate each other, since they both know all the tricks and ploys, and that leaves room for some good, uncluttered exercise between the sheets. Two Scorpios trust each other, and that is rare for the sole Scorpio in a relationship. To the extent that winning fuels an individual Scorpio's lust, this combo may get boring because sex with another, similar Scorpio offers comfort but not challenge.

Scorpio and Sagittarius

Mars, Pluto, and Jupiter are the ruling planets here, and for sheer sexual fun, which Scorpio is capable of, this combo is hot. Scorpio's darker preoccupations do not cut the mustard with Sag, because she is too busy moving around and looking for the party. Both signs have strong libidos and share senses of humor. Scorpio's verbal zingers have no effect on Sag because she, in her frank way, replies, "Too bad," and moves on. This is a hot combo for the short or long term.

> **When Stars Align**
> The feeling of possessing someone sexually is a major turn-on for Scorpios. They want their partners to be riveted on them for the time they are together. If the relationship moves toward a commitment, expect a high degree of jealousy.

Scorpio and Capricorn

The Scorpion and the Goat are a potent combo. The water signs are very compatible with earth signs, and this combo is probably the most sexually hot. Scorpio respects Capricorn because of his work ethic and commitment to power and success. Both signs do not reveal themselves easily, and peeling away the layers of artifice will be as interesting as peeling away layers of clothing before you hit the bed. Mars and Pluto, Scorpio's rulers coupled with Saturn, may, for a long-term commitment, get a bit dour, but for a short-term relationship, they have a strong sexual charge.

Scorpio and Aquarius

These two powerhouse signs are in the not-so-hot astrological relationship called the square. Their elements are water and air. When Aquarius is in his electrifying marathon-sex phase, Scorpio and he will have a worthy, sexy battle between their equally intense signs. Scorpio, however, can control when he turns off and on, whereas Aquarius is at the mercy of his Uranian impulses and short attention span. Scorpio does not like the unpredictability of Aquarius. Both sides can be extreme sexual experimenters, but at the end of the night, this combo wears thin because Scorpio is all about possession, and Aquarius wants to be available to everyone.

Scorpio and Pisces

This is perhaps the most interesting relationship between two signs of like elements, water and water. It is hot, nurturing, fun, and challenging in the short or long term. Pisces is the only sign that Scorpio cannot manipulate. When Scorpio tries to dominate or assert his power on Pisces, the Fish swims away and waits for the tide to change. There is no fight, no scene, just a shimmer of Pisces's vague charm that leaves Scorpio to fight with himself. That usually proves uninteresting, so the seduction begins again. These two can go on in this way for a lifetime and feel very satisfied and compatible.

Sex Planets: Mars and Venus

When a planet is in the sign of Scorpio, the intensity and passion of Scorpio influences that planet. Certain planets can take it and certain ones can't. Take a look at the following placements to learn more about yourself and your partner and how Scorpio operates.

Mars in Scorpio

Scorpio is the ruler of Mars along with Pluto. Pluto was discovered in the beginning of the nuclear age. In mythology, Pluto was god of the underworld and ruled over the souls sent down below. The transformative power that nuclear power unleashes symbolizes the metamorphosis that Scorpio lives daily. With these two powerful planets, Mars and Pluto, ruling Scorpio, you can imagine that Mars in Scorpio is an intense and hot placement. Even if this is the only Scorpio planet in a person's chart, the effect will be palpable.

There is a decidedly thrill-seeking tendency with this placement. Motorcycles, bungee jumps, and dangerous sex all are appealing. Think about nipping into a dark alley for a quickie, and Mars in Scorpio will know just the right one. The danger fuels the pleasure.

Venus in Scorpio

The mild-mannered, peace-loving planet of Venus is not considered well placed in Scorpio. Venus is too small and sweet to easily manifest the boiling passion of Scorpio. The person with this placement is always trying to juggle the good and bad angels of her nature.

Sexually speaking, she is hot, but with this placement, the abandon that she might feel is inhibited. Also, the meaner emotions, such as jealousy and vengeance, can create havoc in relationships. Scorpio is powerful even if it is in a placement that is not conducive to allowing its full strength.

> **Written in the Stars**
> People who have this placement in an otherwise milder chart are often surprised at the intensity of their feelings. Using this power creatively avoids the excesses in food, alcohol, drugs, or sex that Scorpio may indulge in.

Whether a man or woman has Venus in Scorpio, there is a tendency to dress provocatively, sometimes even sexier than the person actually is. The pose of sexiness may be more interesting to Venus in Scorpio than the reality.

Chapter 9

Sagittarius
(November 22–December 21)

Sagittarius may begin life as the happy-go-lucky gambler and then in middle age become more interested in philosophy and knowledge. His libido will remain strong no matter what; he just may be a bit choosier about partners in later life. This sign, above all others, will be very clear about his intentions. Sagittarius is uncomfortably frank, even blunt. Water signs (and Leo), who prefer truth candy coated, must watch out, because they will not get strokes unless Sagittarius means it.

The Adventurer

The ninth sign of the zodiac, Sagittarius is not quite human and not all animal. The symbol for Sagittarius is the Archer, a centaur (a creature that is half horse and half man) that carries a long bow. The dichotomy between man and beast means that there can be two very different types of Sagittarians. The first is a party animal, a roving, restless sort who gambles, laughs deeply, and is happy to have sex with anyone whom he comes across. His goal in sex is exclusively pleasure, not conquest or dominance. The more mature and evolved Sagittarian shoots his arrows into the realm of philosophy and ideas and wants to know about people's thoughts.

"Let's go on an adventure" is the Sagittarian's middle name. Whether she is walking down the street for a loaf of bread or sizing up the possibilities of getting someone into bed, Sag considers everything an adventure. When this attitude is coupled with sex, the result is usually terrifically enjoyable. Sagittarius is the most good-natured sign of the zodiac, and her fiery nature is predisposed to friendly sex. She is enthusiastic by nature, and when this energy is directed toward the bedroom, the result can be irresistible.

The trick with Sagittarius is to pin him down long enough to get to the bedroom. Sag is in love with motion, and so restless that he may fly somewhere to find that person he used to know who had that unbelievable talent with their lips. He loves exploring different cultures, and travel is necessary for him. Looking for partners in the four corners of the world might be a lifelong adventure and occupation for Sag.

His sexual curiosity is strong, and he has a very quick tempo. Once is usually not enough. Since most Sagittarians are quite athletic, they look for a partner who is fit and has sexual staying power. Sagittarius may not enjoy lazing around as part of sex.

Sagittarius is adventurous in trying new and unusual sexual positions, but will shun anything to do with sex toys or paraphernalia. These things, in Sag's opinion, only get in the way of a good time.

Passion Points
The thighs and butt are areas that catch Sag's fancy. Their legs will usually be well developed and very muscular, good for holding on tight and riding a partner like the wind.

What Turns Sagittarius On—and Off

Rather than any one technique or body part, Sagittarius is turned on by exuberance. He may be clumsy in pursuit. In other words, he can easily trip on the way to the boudoir, or spill marinara sauce on his top at dinner, but his sheer willingness and delight in exploring his partner's world overcomes any faux pas. He is like an eager puppy, and when you are the object of his kisses, hugs, and enthusiasm, you will feel caught up in a whirl of passion.

Sagittarians tend to be either tall and slim or short and compact. Tall Sagittarians definitely find legs the sexiest part of a partner's body, and the short ones tend to concentrate just on the thighs. Female Archers like tall partners with whom they can run and play. Any partner who is not prepared for rough-and-tumble sex would be better off choosing a quieter sign.

Vocal expression and silly sounds are mating calls for Sag. At the high point of passion, he may trumpet his pleasure loud enough for anyone in the vicinity to hear. You might want to keep music on at all times. Before the crucial moment, Sag will repeat nonsense syllables and endearments just for the pleasure of expressing his joy.

Turnoffs for Sag all come under the category of superficial and artificial behavior. If she feels manipulated or BS-ed, there will be no relationship—sexual or otherwise. Compliments are fine, but stroking the ego only to get her into bed will backfire. Sags usually know their worth.

Other turnoffs are overly wet kisses and too much saliva on various body parts before getting into bed. It is strange, but as lusty as Sag is, she sometimes does not like to be touched before she is actually in a sexual situation. This is part of her restlessness; perhaps it is because it feels to her as if someone is trying to corral her before she has the impulse to get between the sheets.

The last and biggest turnoff is a possessive, moody, marriage-come-hell-or-high-water partner. In fact, this combination of character traits will probably mean that Sag will never move beyond "Hello, how do you do?" It is easy to be attracted to Sag. If you want to move to more, couch your agenda in "let's have an adventure together" terms and never make her feel lassoed.

Sagittarius's Strengths and Specialties

Variety is Sag's great strength. You will never get bored with the Archer. Having sex in different locations is one way of keeping the fires burning. A permanent suite at the airport where you and your Sag partner can watch the planes taking off could be the sexiest place on earth. A Sagittarian probably invented the mile-high club. If you live in a small town and there aren't many anonymous places where you can exercise your libido, then Sag will take you on an adventure right at home...with imagination. Role-playing is a natural seduction and sex technique with Sag. Sagittarius has many philosophical and religious interests. The moral aspect of religion is usually too confining and limiting for Sag to bother with because he believes that sex is holy and a sacrament to participate in religiously. If this scenario doesn't interest you, Sag will change easily and quickly.

Physically robust, Sag is ready for sex whenever and wherever. She has no particular down or up time;

when the mood comes, she's available. In fact, sex can be Sag's secret weapon. It feels good and diverts from messy questions about the future. If you feel insecure in your relationship with a Sag and feel that any question about "forever" winds up very satisfyingly in the bedroom, ask a direct question. Do not assume that good sex means a committed relationship.

> ☀ **Written in the Stars**
> Sag loves warm and spicy scents. Wafting a cinnamon or nutmeg scent in the room or on the pillows will enflame Sag's enthusiasm.

Sagittarius's Weaknesses and Foibles

Sagittarius is not the most suave or diplomatic sign of the zodiac. She is so connected to calling it like she sees it that her compliments may seem backhanded. And if you ask her opinion on something, be prepared to receive her very frank answer. She is incapable of dressing up the truth. Avoid the questions "Do I look fat?" or "How is my hair?" The answer may make you wince, even though it is intended to be supportive and helpful. The same warning stands for questions about bedroom technique and success or failure. Sag will tell you, "That wasn't so good, let's try this." Or she might say boldly, "Do it this way" and give you very clear instructions for what she wants. She believes in educating partners and herself so that you can both forget mental preoccupations and abandon yourselves to sensations.

The very changeability and love of travel that some partners find so attractive in Sag can be her greatest weakness. You have to work hard to pin her down, even to have that first sexual encounter. She is not being coy, just true to her nature. This zooming-around tendency will not stop even if you are happily married for one hundred years. Sag needs to experience the world and learn things every day. If she is curtailed from this, she can become violently temperamental and use her passion to tell you off in no uncertain terms.

The Sagittarius Man

In the bedroom, he is happy to initiate and happy to try out a great new technique he heard of from a Nepalese shaman. He doesn't go in for foreplay much, because he feels it is slow and boring. After he kisses you, gives you a few playful rubs on the bottom, and shows his appreciation of your thighs and belly, you two are good to go. The Sag man doesn't have a plan. He follows his instincts, which have been well honed for thousands of years. Getting physical is, for Sag, the most pleasurable way of exchanging information and learning. For this period of time, his adventure is you.

Sag can be successful in a variety of professions, but doesn't believe that he needs success to get a partner attracted to him. He assumes it, because all his life people have been attracted to him. All he needs in his professional life is respect and motion. He never equates money and power with sex.

Sagittarian men and women both suffer from foot-in-mouth disease. In men, it usually manifests itself in two ways: an inability to keep a secret, and a way of tossing off remarks that are meant to help but instead usually wound the listener. A Sag man tells secrets because he wants to share the truth. His motivation is not duplicity, but you cannot trust him with information that you don't want made public. There is no cure for the foot-in-mouth tendency. Fortunately, Sag has so many other good traits that his friends forgive him.

> **Written in the Stars**
> Velvet comforters, robes, or drapes around your bed give Sagittarius the feeling of occasion and importance that he loves. Emphasize the colors wine, evergreen, or purple. Do not, however, totally close drapes around the bed. Sagittarians need a sense of space to feel free.

The Sagittarius Woman

These on-the-go women are vital and vivacious. They attract partners easily, and if they are interested in keeping them, they can do that also. Part of a Sag woman's charm is that she is not interested in the way life works, but instead is passionately devoted to life as it should be. She believes in opportunities for everyone. She worships fun and adventure, and she wants to gobble up as much experience as she can. She is usually funny and not put off by anyone's quirks unless they involve lying and deceit.

Written in the Stars

The best gift for a Sag woman is a set of totally practical luggage. The second-best gift is travel tickets for two to a secret rendezvous.

The Sagittarian woman is eager to please sexually. She initiates sex only when she feels her partner matches her ardor. On top, on the bottom, playing the virgin or the whore, a Sag woman wants to exercise her sexual creativity. She likes sex and does not use it for manipulation. A Sag woman's way of getting what she wants is to disappear. Then, when you feel the energy drop because your optimist has left and you are panting for her, she'll come back, and you forget what the argument between you was.

Sag women like an environment of creative chaos around them. In her bedroom, she is apt to keep her special, sexy camisoles draped on the chair to grab quickly, and a few packages of peanuts in her underwear drawer in case you get hungry after sex. Convenience dominates her thinking, rather than an environment that is "as it should be." She does not go out of her way to be unconventional, but if, in the rush of exploring life, her sneakers end up hanging on the coat rack, at least they are there in plain sight when she wants to take a jog or run toward you.

> **Written in the Stars**
> A Sag woman is bold in terms of not only what happens between partners but where. A quickie is not unusual, and if the urge comes while you are driving down the highway, pull over, get that blanket out, and let nature take its course.

The tendency to speak before thinking afflicts Sagittarian women also. Sagittarian women gossip but with a moral proviso that goes like this: "I am not sure, but I heard thus and so. Do you believe it?" The rumor is already cooking, and Sagittarius is oblivious to her contribution. Sagittarian women are also proficient in trying to be helpful but usually saying something hurtful. Again, their charm and honesty always save them, and no one holds this tendency against them.

Setting the Scene

Let's go on a Sagittarian sex adventure. Imagine the motion of a team of horses pulling a pleasure palace on wheels. There is no sound but the rocking of the tent and the creak of the wheels. Inside, Sagittarius is eating grapes by tossing them up and catching them in his mouth or maybe dancing behind a series of scarves. You are delighted. Remember, there is that rocking-horse motion continually. Then, Sagittarius takes his scimitar and cuts the sash holding the curtains around the bed, and the two of you are rocking as well. With each different passing landscape, you and your partner change positions: up, down, and sideways.

Translating this scene to modern (and perhaps more convenient) times is simple for Sagittarius. All that is required is a short trip somewhere, a room with lots of space and air, and a big bed. A round bed would intrigue a Sagittarian. Light a candle if you want some instant atmosphere, and then go for it. It doesn't matter if there is noise outside, an alarm clock that goes off, or a telephone that rings. Sagittarius will kick it away and go right on doing what he is good at.

Sexy Matches: The Hot and Not-So-Hot Combinations

Sagittarius is an incredibly optimistic sign that puts most of the zodiac naysayers to shame. If you find that you are hot for one of the not so hots, it is very possible that the Sagittarian cheerfulness will win over, and you both will have a great time. Love, enthusiasm, and desire can make a good combo with almost anyone.

Sagittarius and Aries

These two fire signs together are like two peas in a pod or, better yet, like two fireflies in summer. They glow and spark off each other. Their strong points are flowing with quick changes of scenery or mind and great senses of humor. Both are daring and will court quickies and sex in risky places. A small chance of getting caught lends spice to the experience. A standing position is fun for these two because they are usually strong physically. And the happiest part of a love affair with Aries and Sagittarius is that they can match each other's energy because they speak the same fiery language. Sag is more philosophical, restless, and worldly by nature—but what the heck, he can adapt if Aries wants to stick near the barbecue and pop into the tool shed for an afternoon romp.

Sagittarius and Taurus

These two signs are fire and earth, and have two very different qualities. Sagittarius is a mutable (or changeable) sign, and Taurus a fixed sign. The tempo of these signs is too problematic to be hot. Sag is speedy and never where you expect her to be, and Taurus is slow and dependable. When they actually get to Taurus's place (because Sag's is usually too far away or too eccentrically decorated for Taurus) they may have a good time. Sag likes the attention Taurus can lavish on her, and Sag's ardor teases the Bull. This combo is very good for a work relationship; they can be lucky together. If some of that success spills over into sex, it is a good deal for a short time.

Sagittarius and Gemini

Opposites attract, and this fire and air combination ruled by Jupiter and Mercury is inspirational. These are both restless signs and sexual daredevils. If Gemini proposes one of her outlandish ideas, Sag will be ready before she can finish the sentence. Their common quality of mutability is a major turn-on. Also, both signs are happy to get physical in any and all locations. The oral skill of Gemini combined with the thrusting power of Sagittarius is a hot combo.

> **When Stars Align**
> Sagittarius can become very angry if he feels thwarted either by reality when he is in a fanciful mood or by someone dampening his enthusiasm. The reaction is like a child when a favorite toy is taken away. He hollers and shouts and needs to isolate himself until his customary good mood returns.

Sagittarius and Cancer

Jupiter and the Moon are friendly planets with each other, but in this case, Jupiter increases Cancer's emotions, and that is not hot between them. Sagittarius laughs at Cancer's emotional sensitivity, which sometimes gets the Crab to stop whining. But when they get to bed, Cancer needs more gentle handling than Sag is willing to give. The fire-and-water combo here douses enthusiasm, and Sag cannot stand that. This combination is not so hot at the end of the night.

Sagittarius and Leo

The fire brotherhood continues with Leo and Sagittarius. They meet and are a hot combo because of their common element. However, Sag may have to take a vow of silence and not respond to Leo's desire for compliments. Sag cannot candy coat the truth, and Leo cannot bear to be challenged by a statement that shows him to be less than magnificent. Sex with a gag on Sag's mouth could work beautifully. Also, Sagittarius may tire of Leo's need for attention and feel that the Archer's unique charm is not getting due attention. If so, Sagittarius will walk away after a few encounters, and will be glad for the experience but not eager for an encore.

Sagittarius and Virgo

A square relationship between fire and earth is known astrologically as a challenging relationship. There is an element of mystery between these two signs that can make for hot sex and for a long-term relationship. They live in different worlds, and Sag gets off on exploring other cultures. The details Virgo loves drive Sag mad, but when these details are part of planning a night of sex, Sag is happy to go along. For just a fling, the obstacles between the two may become a drag. Sag does not enjoy the critical Virgo approach to sexual harmony. Long term, with one person (Virgo) in charge of the details, and the Sagittarian handling the big picture, this combination can get a lot done.

Sagittarius and Libra

Fire and air and two lucky ruling planets (Jupiter and Venus) make this a hot combination. Sagittarius loves to tease Libra and recount the wild sexual exploits he has managed. Libra protests, falsely squeals, and fools Sag into thinking that Libra hasn't mussed up the sheets a number of times. This relationship is hot because both parties are so charming and eager for sex and romance. A Sag may be hotter than a Libra, but Libra is happy to learn; and a Sag may be more daring than a Libra, but since Sagittarius is the sign of the teacher, it all works out just fine.

Sagittarius and Scorpio

Fire and water are the elements, and the planetary combination is Jupiter and Mars. This combination is hot. Both signs are into sex and like to express themselves physically. Still, this will always be a slightly unusual relationship because Scorpio's intense, private nature and sometimes covert tactics are anathema to Sagittarian openness and frankness. The Archer and the Scorpion live in different moral universes: Sag trying to understand the big picture, and Scorpio trying to fathom the depths. Kinky scenarios and concentration on the backside may be the areas of maximum pleasure for this lusty combination.

Sagittarius and Sagittarius

What happens when the planet of generosity and
expansion, Jupiter, meets another Jupiterian? You
have a fantastic party, with philosophical discussions
into the night, all different sorts of people and cultures mingling around, and in that huge bedroom
with the king-sized bed, you have two very ardent,
curious, cheerful people making themselves even
cheerier. The double whammy of these signs is a major turn-on, and these two people can create a center
of joy that will attract many other people. While they
are caught up in traveling and sex and talking and
sex and learning and sex, they are not likely to find
other partners. If one of the combo needs some private space, this will rock the Sagittarian, who wants
to keep the party going.

Sagittarius and Capricorn

Jupiter, Sagittarius's ruler, is the planet of expansion.
Saturn, Capricorn's ruler, is the planet of contraction.

These very different dynamics require a lot of compromise and mature understanding of each other to forge any kind of relationship. A casual fling is possible because both signs are fond of social and sexual interaction. Pushing away any thoughts of living together, working together, or being lifelong friends, Sag and Capricorn meet in lust. The animal half of the Archer is hot for that horny Capricorn Goat, but the basic dichotomy between the signs is wearing for anything longer than a midnight encounter.

Sagittarius and Aquarius

This is a surprising combo because the Sagittarian fire heats up Aquarian coolness, and Aquarius feels comfortable with Sagittarius's integrity and easy good nature. The experimental side of Sag finds a willing partner in Aquarius. The only drawback is that when Aquarius is turned off, Sag will become frustrated by his inability to get things going. Sag does not have energy dips the way Aquarius does and will take it personally if the lights go out. The absolute assurance between Aquarius and Sag that no one's freedom will be curtailed by a liaison between them is a great turn-on.

Sagittarius and Pisces

Before the discovery of Neptune (Pisces's ruler), Pisces was ruled by Jupiter, and today, Pisces is still considered to be co-ruled by the planet of expansion and generosity. That means that Sag and Pisces share some Jupiterian traits. The signs are in different elements, fire and water, which don't normally blend sexually, but here the outlook on life can be so in tune that elemental foibles don't matter as much. By giving each other lavish attention to the feet and legs, both Sag and Pisces will be swimming in oceans of pleasure.

Sex Planets: Mars and Venus

Any Sun sign can have their Mars or Venus in a different sign. To understand more about your partner, figure out in what sign his or her Venus and Mars are located. Sagittarius, ruled by Jupiter, expands and "positivizes" any planet he contacts.

Mars in Sagittarius

Mars is a fiery planet, and in Sagittarius, he finds a compatible sign for his energy. Sag's ruling planet, Jupiter, also ennobles the more raucous demonstrations of Mars's aggression. Sexually, this position is uncomplicated. Stimulus equals response equals release. Mars in Sag wants to express his fire and is happy with anyone who wants to go along with him. The passions with Mars in Sag also include discussions of philosophy and ways that an individual can create a more productive life. There is no conflict with Sag in moving from high-minded thoughts to low-minded lust. Remember that the symbol is half animal and half man. Both aspects of living deserve expression in Sagittarians' worlds.

This sign can be a prankster and has no inhibitions about playing sexual games with favorite partners.

Roller-skating to a first date while dressed in a tuxedo or nipping into a private box at the opera for a quickie is Mars in Sag's idea of sexy fun and humor.

Both men and women with this sign enjoy horses and being around horses. Plan a weekend retreat to the track, and you will see anyone with this placement shed his propriety and become an enthusiastic gambler. The flush of enthusiasm floods over to the bedroom. Whinnying and neighing with pleasure, your Mars in Sag will take her riding crop, spur you on to great pleasure, and then run the race again and again.

Venus in Sagittarius

Although not as demonstrative as Mars in Sagittarius, Venus is comfortable in this fire sign. The coupling of Venus and Jupiter signs always means good luck. Good luck in sexual relations translates into pleasure. The partners have easy communication and don't let their minds get in the way of a good time.

A peculiarity of this placement is that Venus in Sagittarius is usually early for dates. Even though Venus in Sag rushes around with the breakneck speed typical of all Sag placements, when it comes to a love tryst, she tends to let her enthusiasm lead her and be waiting for her partner. If she is really hot, which is easy for her to be, she won't bother with even hello. Just open the door, fall on the bed, and go to it.

A person with Venus in Sagittarius will attract a partner who is casual, sports minded, physically fit, and interested in different sexual experiments. Women and men with this position can be very fair-minded leaders and artists and want an equal for a partner or mate. They pride themselves on taking care of themselves and being independent. Leaning on a partner and sitting by the telephone wishing they would call is not in the playbook.

Chapter 10

Capricorn
(December 22–January 19)

Capricorn is an earth sign and is ruled by Saturn. Saturn was the farthest planet that the ancients knew about and was called the planet of discipline, structure, and time. The god Saturn was not considered a cheery fellow, and in the present day, Capricorns have a tendency to worry and look on the more somber side of life. Sex can do a lot to alleviate this tendency.

The Pragmatist

Capricorn's symbol is a goat climbing up a mountain. Goats are legendary in all of classical mythology and literature for their horny behavior and omnivorous appetites. Although Capricorn is a very lusty sign, he does not want to be perceived as yearning or too eager. Part of Capricorn's charm is the self-discipline he can maintain. His exterior may be cool, but passion lies underneath.

The mountain that the goat climbs symbolizes success, and Capricorn wants to be successful in all endeavors—including sex. Since people usually don't get medals or public recognition for being good partners, your Capricorn mate wants to know in detail how he rates. He is a pragmatist, after all, and wants to see what works and what doesn't. The sign is not prudish and can be very interested in the particulars of whether this position or that technique was as good as the one the night before.

What Turns Capricorn On—and Off

The single biggest turn-ons for Capricorn are laughter and structured sexual play. You don't have to memorize a manual or announce what will happen next, but in the bedroom, as in life, Capricorn wants to know what is coming. She may like to create a game plan for sex and may spend a lot of time planning exactly how she will go about seduction and lovemaking. Capricorn does not like surprises, and feels spontaneous only when things begin according to plan. Ritual is part of Capricorn's nature, and if you and your partner develop a pleasing way of beginning each date, then the familiarity will encourage trust and hotter sex.

There is a tendency with the Capricorn partner to be very goal oriented. Foreplay is nice, kissing is good, but the main event is the point and goal. However, you will notice that when sex is accompanied by lots of jokes and laughter beforehand, everything works better. Amid the gaiety, Capricorn usually knows what she wants and can be very direct. With the Saturn ruler, she might take a while to heat up, but then the situation looks very good for a satisfying conclusion.

Passion Points

Capricorn rules all bones and the skeletal structure. That is not traditionally a sexy part of the body, but keep in mind unattractive knees or scaly elbows will be a definite turnoff for a Capricorn partner.

Oral sex is a definite turn-on for Capricorn but is less sexy than the main event. In his pursuit of excellence, a Capricorn partner may spend a lot of time working on coming at the same time as his partner. Could be a great time getting there!

Goats like to bite and butt their horns together. Although Saturn is a planet of controlled discipline and energy, there is lots of aggressive power here. It is a turn-on for Capricorn to get his kicks by love biting and playful fighting. This fuels his lust and can easily turn into a tickling fest or a wild pillow fight. Whether you like it fierce or tender, Capricorn likes that kind of sexual cavorting.

The turnoffs for Capricorn are unpredictable emotional displays that interfere with pleasure. She also doesn't want a lot of flirting and beating around the bush. Capricorn has enough pressure, with all the worries and stresses of the world on her shoulders, so when it is party time in the bedroom, abandoning the chattering mind and getting down to business are the point.

Capricorn is turned off by irresponsibility. If she always has to make the arrangements, the where and when of it all, she will feel that her partner isn't doing their part. Her response may be to become very aggressive in bed and then find another partner. She will, however, always take the initiative about safe sex (and, if applicable, birth control). Capricorn is also loath to participate in sex that is less than private. This is not a sign prone to popping into a large closet for a quickie. In order to let go, there must be a safe and structured space, and then Capricorn will feel open and interested.

Capricorn's Strengths and Specialties

Capricorn is (as a rule) a physically strong sign and happy to lend his robust energy to athletic lovemaking. Capricorn is also a yin, or feminine, sign, and there is great receptivity and sensitivity to this sign. He will understand if his partner is not in the mood, but by the strength of his desire, soon enough the juices will be flowing, and you both will be having a fine time.

If you have proclivities for discipline or bondage scenarios, Capricorn could be well suited to this form of sexual expression. It is not a kinky sign, but it can understand the appeal of discipline and the attraction of one partner (that is, the Capricorn) being the boss and calling the shots. Spanking as part of playful fun could be a definite part of Capricorn's sexuality.

Another strength is that Capricorn tends to be a responsible sign. A connection with this person will either lead to a relationship or it won't. He doesn't usually enjoy relationships that are hazy and ill-defined. Capricorn is usually faithful, and if he gives a promise, he keeps it. Before a promise is given, though, he is interested in playing the field.

Written in the Stars
Remember to keep your activities structured, and you will please your Capricorn partner.

Capricorn, an earth sign, has his feet on the ground. If you are held by or hold a Capricorn, you feel his solidity. A kiss is on target and not sloppy. Caresses are definite, and if you ask him to scratch your back, he will find the exact spot that needs scratching. The sign is also a dependable partner. If you have mentioned to your Capricorn partner that you like having Cool Whip all over your body, then you can be sure that there will be Cool Whip at your next meeting, and the next, and the next...until you say that your taste has changed.

Capricorn's Weaknesses and Foibles

Capricorn is not usually an early-morning partner. She usually sleeps heavily, and if the morning is your best time, you may have a bit of trouble getting desire going. At night, Capricorn will leave the day's cares and happily stay in the bedroom or on the living room couch. Capricorns do not tend to be very vocal partners and do not indulge in pet names and sweet words. If you hear a shout at the appropriate moment from Capricorn, it will be surprising and satisfying for both of you.

The very same goal orientation and love of structure that makes Capricorn successful in the world can, in the bedroom, cramp a more spontaneous sign's style. Capricorn can become a slave to habit and "the usual way." He doesn't want to be surprised or feel he is in competition with a more adventuresome partner.

It worries him and spoils the fun. If Capricorn is too careful and cautious because he doesn't want to make a mistake, he won't enjoy a sense of surrender and release.

The Capricorn Man

The word *horny*, meaning "easily aroused," comes from the horns of a goat. The connection fits the Capricorn man. He has a strong sex drive. The Capricorn man first wants passion and sex, and then affection. It is a sign that is mindful of the status of his partner. A major turn-on for a Capricorn guy is being with someone classy but still fun in the bedroom. Capricorn men value decorum and a partner who dresses tastefully and usually conservatively.

Capricorn men will not make the first move unless they are 99 percent sure of success. With the water signs, such as Cancer and Pisces, men don't make the first move because they may be too sensitive and won't easily recover from a rebuff. The Capricorn man is tougher, but doesn't put time and energy into pursuit unless there is a very good chance of having the sexual encounter he desires. The Cap man is happy with seduction, but not teasing. He is the pragmatist; getting all of those feelings and yearnings stirred up means something has to happen.

> **Passion Points**
> The back of the knee will be an especially tender spot.

The Capricorn man's shoulders will undoubtedly be very tight, and massage to help melt away the worries is a great way to begin a fun and satisfying evening. The jaw is also an area where Capricorns hold tension. Kissing, earlobe sucking, and a little biting are good ways to set the agenda for sex. Most Capricorn men work out or consider physical fitness part of their assets. This is usually a turn-on for their partner.

The Capricorn Woman

Here you may find that feeling sexual takes more time than with some other signs. Saturn's rule emphasizes the responsibility aspect of any relationship, and Cap women may feel aroused but cautious. If a Capricorn woman throws caution to the winds though, passion is no stranger to her. Wooing is important to her, and she does not care for a partner who appears too eager. Capricorn wants to be coaxed and doesn't like panting demands. Sensual caresses around the neck, shoulders, and back will make her melt.

She will also create a hospitable room or place for her love affairs. A Capricorn woman loves sensual textures, and making love on a fur comforter would be a wonderful experience for both people. She is not as dependent on atmosphere as other signs but loves the feel of luxurious materials.

Gifts of lingerie could be ivory or black with classic lines. Capricorn women usually have very good bone structure and look good in tailored suits with a white blouse open to show just the right amount of cleavage. A Capricorn woman also looks great in leather. It brings out her tough side, and the combination of tailored outerwear, ivory satin lingerie, and boots is a spicy turn-on.

Setting the Scene

Capricorn wants to enter a timeless realm with her partner: no clocks and no deadlines. A bed with velvet brown or magenta curtains surrounding it becomes a grotto of delight. One candle is all that Capricorn needs to feel desire. Decorate your bedroom with earth colors and keep some rose quartz nearby; Capricorn loves beautiful minerals. Both Capricorn and partner should hide work clothes and any reminders of work, duty, and obligations.

You come into this grotto of sex wearing just pajama tops or perhaps one of you is wearing a kimono. No fooling around with subtleties; just pull them off and hit the sheets. Capricorn is the boss, and the boss says, "now." Maybe after things are a little calmer, there is time for more subtle experiences, like shoulder rubs and kissing that little sexy tense spot in your lower back. But nothing feels better in this grotto than the tension and release of sex. Burn some sage or sandalwood incense to wrap you and your partner in a world of pleasure. Now that you're in a pleasure mode, you have all the time in the world.

Sexy Matches: The Hot and Not-So-Hot Combinations

Knowing the characteristics of your sign and those of your partner can give you an idea of how compatible you'll be. But sexual compatibility can be a complicated thing. If you're unhappy about one of the not-so-good combinations, you may defy the odds. Enjoy the journey and see where life takes you.

Capricorn and Aries

There is no follower here. Both Capricorn and Aries want to lead, and their elements, fire and earth, do not blend easily. Relationships may prove to be combative, but for a fling, the heat of Aries with the staying power of Capricorn could be exhilarating. The fight between the two signs is sexy, and the Ram and the Goat butting heads means a battle of equals. The relationship may not involve more than attraction, with no promises and no demands.

Capricorn and Taurus

These are two earth signs—sensual and grounded, and tuned in to the pleasures of beautiful scents, tastes, and rhythmic lovemaking. This is a good combination for sex, communication, and fun. Capricorn and Taurus are good for a fling, good for a relationship, and good for the long haul. Their sole disadvantage is that they may fall into a rut over time and need some racy DVDs or edible underwear to get desire rekindled. Theirs is a trine relationship, and there is a harmonious flow of energy between the signs in all areas. There is a safe feeling between Capricorn and Taurus, and whatever the partners feel ripples throughout their bodies and is easily communicated to the other. Kisses and rubs around the neck and shoulders could be a religious experience for Taurus and Capricorn.

Capricorn and Gemini

This is neither a sexy combo nor a match made in heaven. Saturn (the ruler of Capricorn) and Mercury (the ruler of Gemini) have different speeds. Thus, Gemini is quick and changeable; Capricorn is slow and methodical. You can imagine the different sexual appetites. Also, Gemini likes lots of talk, sweet words, and oral emphasis of all kinds. Capricorn goes for the full-body sensation and is not as interested in sexy words. One night together could be dizzyingly interesting for Capricorn, but the experience might feel like eating fast food: an hour later, you're hungry again. Earth wants more solid contact and is impatient with Gemini's changeability.

Capricorn and Cancer

This earth and water combination views life, sex, and everything else very differently, but opposites attract and there is attraction between the two signs. It is a fertile combination, so, if this applies to you, be mindful of birth control if you are not in the mood for pregnancy. Capricorn gives Cancer solidity, and Cancer gives Capricorn nurturing and a warm place to cuddle up. Though the sexual chemistry between these two signs is usually tender and sweet, it can lead to fireworks. Capricorn may pull away from Cancer because Cancer will inevitably feel very emotional after sex, and Capricorn does not like to deal with sentiment.

Capricorn and Leo

Earth and fire is the locomotive combination. Leo is the fiery spark that can ignite the earthy Capricorn, and, like a train, the forward motion can chug on forever. The trick here is to have enough connection to ignite the spark.

> **Passion Points**
> The small of the back is a particular erogenous zone for both Leo and Capricorn.

Capricorn and Leo want such different things in life that they may not cross each other's paths. If they do meet, these two signs are demanding sexual partners and will perhaps have a fling and not worry about forever.

Capricorn and Virgo

Earth to earth is a sensual and sexual combination. Capricorn calms Virgo's critical tendency with her determined and steady physicality. This combination enjoys time in the bathtub or hot tub, or a spa rendezvous. Both signs can be modest, but if they believe that they are doing something good for their health, their self-consciousness melts away. Sesame oil massages and salt rubs will set the stage for sensuality nicely.

Capricorn and Libra

This is not one of the easy connections. Libra is air and ruled by Venus; Capricorn is earth and ruled by Saturn. Venus wants to play, flirt, tease, and be the queen or king, and Capricorn says, "Let's get serious." The superficiality that some Librans have is not a turn-on for Capricorn. The two signs meet in their appreciation of a soft touch. Any rough encounters will turn Libra off and are thought indecorous by Capricorn.

Capricorn and Scorpio

This combination is a doozy! Capricorn's native discipline and Scorpio's lust for in-depth expression of feelings, sensuality, and sexuality make the sky the limit as far as sexual expression. Earth and water are harmonious elements in themselves, but when joined by the Capricorn drive and Scorpio passion, they make a powerful connection. The erogenous zones here are everywhere and everything.

Capricorn and Sagittarius

Here we have a well-meaning connection, but not necessarily a passionate one. Earthy Capricorn wants consistency in sexual encounters, and Sagittarius wants to be free to come and go and make different plans. The Goat loves to be touched all over, but the Archer is finicky and sometimes too restless for long nights of lust. The way to work it out is to use different scents. Sag is wild about cinnamon and other spicy aromas.

Capricorn and Capricorn

What would you guess? This is a solid, dependable, sensual, good connection. Capricorns like the sexiness of feeling their energy strengthened by a fellow Goat. Also, with Saturn people, sexual communication deepens over time. Capricorn will remember kissing the special curve of his body or the spot behind her ear-lobe that starts a night of love. And each time that spot is caressed, it leads to good, comfortable sex.

> **Passion Points**
> The back, shoulders, and bottom are erogenous zones for Capricorns.

Capricorn and Aquarius

Traditionally, earth and air are not perfect matches, but here we have an interesting astrological connection, as Aquarius, before the discovery of the planet Uranus, was ruled by Saturn, Capricorn's ruler. The Aquarius who has Saturn predominant will be like a more talkative Capricorn and interested in all oral forms of expression. This would be a comfortable and exciting partner for Capricorn. However, eccentric Uranus-ruled Aquarius is too unpredictable and liberal for most Capricorns. If they meet one of these electrifying Aquarians, most Capricorns will politely decline their attentions.

Capricorn and Pisces

This combination of earth and water has compatibility and ease. Pisces needs fantasy, and his slippery sensuality confuses Capricorn, but the result is friendly sex and genuine affection. All settings that include water will enhance lovemaking with this combination. Pisces also shares Capricorn's love of fabric and material. Silk sheets and a Tiffany lamp casting a soft glow in the bedroom will bring out the sensual best in these two signs.

Sex Planets: Mars and Venus

To learn more about yourself and your partner, figure out in what sign his or her Venus and Mars are located. This information will add finesse to everything you have learned about your partner's Sun sign.

Mars in Capricorn

Mars in Saturn's sign is considered exalted in astrology. An exalted placement means that the planet gains in strength and stature from his location in a particular sign. Mars, which is usually impetuous, benefits from the sustained, controlled energy of Capricorn. These people have considerable sexual appetites and are very capable partners. They like rough-and-tumble sex, but their rhythm is slow and sensual. Men with this placement will rarely have a problem with premature ejaculation. They are interested in exploring sexual techniques that require self-control. Yoga exercises that enhance sexual pleasure might be something both you and he would enjoy studying.

Venus in Capricorn

Venus placed in the sign of Capricorn is lusty and elegant. The placement can be sly when looking forward to a hot date and enjoys organizing the where, when, and how of a rendezvous. Venus in Capricorn likes status, both in her choice of partners and in how the whole date unfolds.

> **Written in the Stars**
> Women with this placement will find that cypress, sandalwood, cedar, and pine scents enhance their sexual and sensual feelings.

A person with this placement must look good but understated. She does not enjoy flashy, outré fashions. To Venus in Capricorn, a well-tailored business suit looks like a perfect come-on because the difference between dressing for success in the outside world and undressing for sex is alluring. Underneath, Venus in Capricorn (male or female) may be wearing very skimpy underwear, which is all part of a carefully choreographed dance to make sex hot and decorous at the same time.

Chapter 11

Aquarius
(January 20–February 18)

The eleventh sign of the zodiac is the individual and sometimes eccentric Aquarius. Although the symbol for Aquarius is the Water Bearer, a maiden pouring water from a jug, Aquarius is a masculine air sign. These seeming contradictions are of no import to Aquarius. He is on his own path in life, and in his sexuality, he is just as unique. This is the sign of the inventor and genius.

The Eccentric

Not every Aquarian is technically a genius, but there is always one part of their personality that is unique and not part of the status quo. In the game of sex, Aquarius can be as inventive as he is in other parts of his life. Be prepared for the weird, wacky, unusual, and electrifying. This does not mean that Aquarians are kinky. Traditional whips and chains or any other XXX-movie scenario might be too hackneyed for Aquarius. He wants to follow his inventive whims and has the daring and enthusiasm to do it. His imagination is boundless.

When astrology first developed, the farthest planet the ancients could see was Saturn, and Aquarians were thought to be ruled by Saturn. In 1781, the planet Uranus was discovered, and from that time, revolutionary Uranus was considered the ruler of Aquarius. Sometimes, Aquarians will be prone to Capricorn-like conservatism. However, as an air sign, Aquarius in the sexual arena is more influenced by thoughts and fantasy than earthy sensuality. This is a friendly sign, and sex and passion are not the be-all and end-all of life. The idea of sex—thinking about it, talking about it, concocting ways to meet that special someone—will engage this person's very fertile mind. Having sex may feel like an anticlimax because the imagination and fantasy life are so rich.

Sexual affairs may challenge Aquarius to investigate
this new position, that new theory, or perhaps a group
situation. She believes that having a group of friends
is the best part of life, and if that turns into a sexual
situation, it's okay by her. Her sexual energy is electric
in nature, and she can catch the vibes of an interested
party faster than any other sign can.

What Turns Aquarius On—and Off

The major turn-on for an Aquarian is being unconventional. A partner must either enjoy this part of Aquarius's personality or forego the relationship. Sneaking
into the office computer room and having a quickie is
an Aquarian's idea of double pleasure: sex, and a unique
spot to enjoy it. Even if you and your Aquarian are at
home for a quiet date, he will want to entertain the idea
that something unexpected could happen. This is a
sign that might erect a trapeze in the bedroom to see
if hanging upside down would be pleasurable. Spontaneity is a major turn-on. His sexuality is like a lightning bolt, and he can turn it on and off with incredible
speed. When he's on, the effect is electrifying; when he
is turned off, there is no use trying to get him in the

mood. The battery is low, and only when he recharges will there be any action. Aquarians have lots of kinetic or electrical energy. Making love with an Aquarian can give you a jolt, and if you are not up to it, the energy can be upsetting. It is sexy and impersonal at the same time. Because Aquarius's personality is so tuned in to the currents of contemporary media and computers, he is turned on by a multimedia experience. Making love with the stereo, computer, and TV all on at the same time is stimulating for Aquarius.

Knowledge is sexy to Aquarians. Stock a library with books or DVDs, and you and your Aquarian partner may hole up in a cabin for days and not get bored. An obvious turnoff is boring sameness. Also, this is a sign that is open to having multiple partners. For Aquarius, it is all part of the brave new world that they envision, where sensation is paramount, and messy emotional displays minimal.

Passion Points

The wrists and ankles are usually very delicate in male and female Aquarians. Kissing, rubbing, and tickling them are especially intimate activities.

Aquarius's Strengths and Specialties

Being a fixed sign, Aquarius has considerable energy. The Aquarian is interested in learning techniques that will transmit her erratic but electrical sexuality. She might study Reiki or massage to improve circulation and maximize pleasure. A crash course in the sexual positions throughout history would give an Aquarian all sorts of ideas, plus there is the additional pleasure of exploring new cultures. She will feel especially in tune with a partner who is not clinging or demanding. Aquarius cannot be pinned down—her strength is in her ability to be charmingly nonpossessive. Serial monogamy with a few good friends on the side may be the pattern for this sign until she settles down. When she meets a match and commits, she will be faithful.

Another little-known turn-on for Aquarians is having sex in airplanes. This may be difficult to manage in economy class, but if you have the means to arrange for a private jet, then the phrase *flying high* may take on new meaning.

Written in the Stars

Brushing your Aquarian partner's body with your hands can smooth all the erratic thoughts and impulses that may clog his nervous system. Start with your palms and brush the front of the legs, the back, the back of the legs, and the back of the arms. Finish by brushing downward on the chest, then place your hands over his ears and feel how his whole system relaxes. Then, head for the futon.

Aquarius's Weaknesses and Foibles

This sign is not the warmest of the zodiac. They are wonderful friends, but the nitty-gritty of passion is not part of Aquarius's vocabulary. Aquarians are not inhibited, just not superhormonal. Sensations and vibes count a lot with them. Aquarius's nerve endings are so highly charged she can communicate almost telepathically with a partner. Her weakness is that she can turn off her energy at will and can even mentally disconnect while making love. All of a sudden, a more sensual sign such as the water or earth signs may feel abandoned and wonder, "Who turned off the juice?"

Written in the Stars

Aquarius can separate love and sex better than any other sign can. They will be very clear which category you fall into and will not change their minds.

It is difficult to get into a sexy rhythm with Aquarius. She will be hot and passionate for one week and then passionately interested in science fiction or something else for three weeks. If you pretend you are a Martian or create an equally fascinating fantasy sequence, you may maximize your chances of continuing sex. An Aquarius may not always feel comfortable with random touching and silence. Chatting throughout sex and even spinning a wild fantasy while she is doing it might be a cosmic orgasm for Aquarius: it keeps the body and mind percolating together.

The Aquarius Man

Remember the two rulers of Aquarius: Saturn and Uranus. The Aquarian man ruled by Saturn will tend to be more conservative and cautious. He typically will not have the strong sex drive that Capricorn does. He wants a relationship with parameters and a few quirks, for no matter how much Saturn is in his personality, unpredictable Uranus will still affect his attitude. This type of Aquarian will be more dependable and regular about his sexual relationships. He will be tolerant, interested in expanding his mind, and seduced by innuendo rather than sweaty, hot passion.

> **Written in the Stars**
> The clear, crisp air of the mountains in winter is a tonic and turn-on for Aquarius. Consider a vacation at a chalet. After skiing or walking in the cold, plunge into an outdoor hot tub and then run naked into the snow and see what happens.

The Uranus-ruled Aquarian man has a unique place in today's society because he is tuned in to the changing nature of the roles of the sexes. He can grow his hair long and not mind if someone mistakes him for a woman. Being unique is sexy for the Aquarian. This is the man who, on principle, believes that all people should express their sexuality in whatever way they would like, and he may champion those rights. He loves to talk about the possibilities of society coming to terms with messy emotions. He himself does not like to feel messy emotions, and wants his sexuality to be free of the constraints of typical monogamy. In his own relationships, he may not be as liberal as his conversation leads you to think.

> **Written in the Stars**
> Bring your Aquarian man a model airplane as a gift.
> It is offbeat and may wake up the boy inside the
> man.

For the Aquarian man, communication is about sharing ideas and envisioning a better world. If that includes hugging, kissing, and making love, then so much the better. He will enjoy making love after physical exercise because his circulation is primed. Hot and cold showers give him a tingle, and then he is ready to plunge ahead. When things get physical, maintain eye contact with your Aquarian man. He gives and receives energy through the eyes and is highly stimulated when a connection is maintained.

The Aquarian man believes in no inhibitions, but you may find that he is a bit modest when it comes down to being naked with a partner. Don't be afraid to take the lead in sex. Just assure him that he is free, and you will have the best of this very individual sign.

The Aquarius Woman

She is a cool customer. The Aquarian woman is ruled by a yang sign and is also interested in being an iconoclast. She loves to break stereotypes. She may be a tomboy or a sleek fashion model. If she is influenced more by Saturn, then the conflict between her desire to be unique and her wish to maintain the status quo puts her in a sexual bind, and she can stay in a rut for a long time. If passion leads you toward an uptight Aquarian woman and you unleash her potential, you will find a rush of passion that will keep you panting and very excited.

The Aquarian woman loves to have her lower back rubbed. She tends to be physically fit and may be able to do a few pretzel positions that will surprise her partner. She is game to try anything.

Her partners will always be her friends because that is the highest compliment she pays anyone.

Written in the Stars

Brush your Aquarian woman's hair, which will probably crackle with electricity, especially in the winter months.

She will be happy taking the dominant position in lovemaking. She will also be happy in making the first move because, for the Aquarian woman, it is all part of a game that interests her when she is in the mood. Romance is not so important, and atmosphere is also not so important. Communication of like minds that includes physical sensations is important. If this sounds like something Spock from Star Trek might say, realize that Aquarians are future oriented and believe wholeheartedly that passion has led the world into chaos. They, in their own relationships, are trying to right the balance.

Setting the Scene

The room could be anywhere as long as it is unique and there is lots of space and light. High-rise apartments where you and your partner can see the passing clouds are paradise. The walls are white; the décor is spare but inviting. There is a whiff of Tibetan incense in the air and a lava lamp gently pulsing on the side table. In the background, you may hear a soft, reedy melody. Things heat up while you are having an intense conversation about the future of the world. Then, your Aquarian mentions that in the future people will make love by touching each other's thumbs. That idea appeals, and you move from touching thumbs to wrists to kissing up the arms. Then, suddenly, you are both in a reclining position and sure that the future of the world depends on satisfying the feelings between you. As long as the tingly feeling continues, that's how long you and your Aquarian partner will go at it. If one of you lags, then Aquarius will keep her own motor going until things perk up. The sexiest setting for Aquarius is unplanned, unrehearsed sex. It may be erratic, but it is worth waiting for. So, go for it, wherever.

Sexy Matches: The Hot and Not-So-Hot Combinations

Keeping Aquarius's famous cool character in mind, and remembering that sexual chemistry has its own surprising ways, what do you think the sexiest combination would be? The winner is Aquarius and Leo. Read on to see about the other possibilities. As with all the signs, if you disagree with any of the not-so-hot combinations, trust your instincts and go with the flow. By the way, if you feel you (or your partner) are more conservative than the following explanations of Aquarius, consult the combos with Capricorn for a fuller view of the sexy possibilities.

Aquarius and Aries

The elements here are inflammatory, air and fire. The ruling planets of these two signs, Mars and Uranus, are also combustible. An Aquarius is not fazed by Aries's speedy manner and loves the fiery charm. All the fire signs warm Aquarius up, and because Aries does not like routine, she understands when Aquarius pops by at three in the morning and wants to get close. There can be a lot of laughter here, and Mars's straightforward sex appeal can keep up with Aquarius's more unusual sexual appetites. The drawback between the two signs is that Aquarius is not as individually oriented as Aries, and even though they may spark each other's interest, their views of life are very different. For best results, make love by candlelight, even in the daytime.

Sexy videos, TV, rock music, and other extra stimuli are okay with this combination.

Aquarius and Taurus

This combination is the battle of the titans! Both sex signs are enormously willful, and if they have a thing for each other, there will be many negotiations about who does what to whom. Aquarius will talk and Taurus won't listen, but between the sheets, the energy of air and earth could make for profound sexual pleasure...for a time. Aquarius can electrify Taurus out of normal habits, and Taurus gives Aquarius a feel for sensuality that Aquarius does not have naturally. The upper back is the place to begin. This love affair doesn't usually last, but the short-term experience may be liberating for both partners.

Aquarius and Gemini

Air and air are compatible elements, and the surprising nature of both these signs makes them a zesty combination. Both air signs love to talk about sex. This would be the time to try out your phone sex fantasies. Keep a cell phone under your bed, and you both will have fun.

Gemini, ruled by Mercury, loves the teasing that Aquarius, ruled by Uranus, does instinctively. Saying, "I will do this to you" or "If you are very, very good, I will do that" gets Aquarius's fantasy life primed for a physical encounter. The best part of sex with these two signs is that they won't bore each other.

Aquarius and Cancer

This combination could be called cold and hot. It usually results in misunderstanding and frustration for the Aquarian because he does not enjoy Cancer's vast repertoire of emotional responses. Sexually, it is irritating for these two signs to be together, but Aquarius's love of understanding human behavior may keep him in pursuit as he attempts to fathom Cancer's moody language. An Aquarian who wants to get into a Cancerian's boudoir should lavish attention on the breasts or chest, nuzzling, cupping, and appreciating. To really score, Aquarius should approach Cancer at the full moon: if anything wild or weird is going to happen between them, it will happen then.

Aquarius and Leo

This combo is hot, and a great instance of opposites attracting. Leo is probably the most personally centered sign of the zodiac, and Aquarius is the most group centered. Their elements are air and fire, and their ruling planets are Uranus and the Sun. The sexual give-and-take is great because Aquarius appreciates Leo's passion and needs the warmth of the sun, and Leo needs an audience and sparkles in trying to get the approval and energy he needs from Aquarius. They could spend a very successful relationship fighting, making up, and trying to understand each other, all the while having great sex. It can be naughty because both signs can be exhibitionists. At that office party, after they leave a door slightly open, you may catch a glimpse of Leo and Aquarius standing against the wall in a posture that is comfortable for only one thing. Leo and Aquarius should emphasize the spine, rubbing it, massaging it, or turning upside down. And if Aquarius has a tape of audience applause and plays it every time they make love, Leo will definitely be pleased.

Aquarius and Virgo

Different elements (air and earth), and different qualities (fixed and mutable), mean that these two live in different worlds. Looking just at sex, there are some possibilities here because Aquarius is turned on by Virgo's charm and consistency. Aquarius may pursue Virgo to find out what makes this sign tick. Aquarius imagines that Virgo's sexy talk and proper behavior is a cover and underneath Virgo is as unconventional as Aquarius. This is a fantasy. As soon as an Aquarian discovers that Virgo really does like being conventional, the relationship loses its spice.

> **When Stars Align**
> Sleeping together after sex may be too bumpy for these two—have a big bed or, better yet, two doubles side by side.

Aquarius will want a friendship with this lovely creature, and if that means some time in a bedroom that is too clean and orderly for Aquarius's sense of décor, then so be it. This is not usually a lasting combination.

Aquarius and Libra

The friendly and flowing trine relationship between Aquarius and Libra makes this a good, sexy match for a short- or long-term connection. Aquarius loves the romantic and beautiful Libra, and although Libra will usually protest that Aquarius is too different, Libra enjoys the match of wits and the love of mental stimulation they share.

This is an air combination that will love the sound of each other's voice. When it gets down to doing the deed, Aquarius will have to make some effort to keep Libra's romantic fantasy quota filled. Unless there are deeper ties of a commitment, Aquarius might get bored with Libra. Libra is more conventional than Aquarius and does not like exciting or weird sexual positions, but before the "blahs" set in, this will be a stimulating combo.

> ### When Stars Align
> Aquarius's ability to have different partners will not wash at all with Libra. It's best for Aquarius to keep the other "friends" secret, or Libra will be gone, and both will miss out on a charming relationship.

Aquarius and Scorpio

This is a meeting of equals in terms of energy, fixity, and power. Aquarius's fantasy life and everything-is-possible sexuality appeals to Scorpio. This can be a kinky combination with S&M possibilities. Aquarius does not attach any moral judgments to cavorting around in boots or with whips and chains, and Scorpio is simply turned on by the daring that his Aquarian partner shows. The dominance aspect between these two signs can change frequently because Aquarius is erratic and Scorpio needs different stimuli. When you get right down to sex, the energies between these two may be more mentally intriguing than physically satisfying—but what a conclusion to come to! Aquarius and Scorpio will get off on the exploration.

Aquarius and Sagittarius

The combination of the elements of air and fire means that, at last, Aquarius has met a talker that will be able to keep up with her. This combination makes for friendly, compatible sex and lots of motion. These two will do it in a car, train, ship, or wherever. You may find that, in the midst of lovemaking, Sag is talking and Aquarius is listening, and then vice versa. If you focus on using this oral facility in a more physical way, you and your partner will be more than satisfied. Humming a tune while engaged will also increase the vibrations.

> **When Stars Align**
> Aquarius and Sagittarius often share a love of the same colors. Emphasize gifts of clothing in rich blues and greens, and you will be well on your way to having a good time between the sheets.

Sag and Aquarius can be silly and playful together. Sagittarius is also a freedom-loving sign, and Aquarius has no problem with that. Sag will demand total honesty, though, if Aquarius's other "friends" become partners.

Aquarius and Capricorn

If Aquarius is more ruled by Saturn than Uranus, a combination with Capricorn works well. However, the less conventional Aquarians will chomp at the bit when confronted with Capricornian conservatism. Even though their life views are very different, the naked fact of sex can be satisfying. Sexually speaking, Capricorn has more libido than Aquarius has and does not need the fantasizing that Aquarius loves to get going.

Aquarius and Aquarius

This may be a battle of eccentricities—but at least the players understand the beat of the different drummer that rules them both. Sexually speaking, one of the partners may be slightly more Saturnian than the other, and part of the kick of this relationship will be to introduce the more conservative partner to the wild and wacky Aquarian world. Surprise trysts, weekend workshops on kundalini-enhancing postures, as well as sex any irregular way that appeals will be the path to a sexy relationship between these two very individual people. Making love in the shower or the pool may particularly turn on this combination. With all that electrical Aquarian energy, they both might need soft, caressing water to remind them of their feelings.

Aquarius and Pisces

Water and air can create a beautiful bubble relationship, and Pisces loves to feel secure within a cozy world of sensation. However, in general, the frisson between these two signs is short lasting and not satisfying. Different rhythms predominate: Pisces likes to swim in sexual feelings, and Aquarius likes to hop around from one sensation to the other. If you catch each other long enough to get together, concentrate on tickling each other's feet and ankles. It could be the beginning of a short-lived but fun relationship.

Sex Planets: Mars and Venus

To learn more about yourself and your partner, figure out in which sign his or her Venus and Mars are located. This information will add zing to everything you have learned about your partner's Sun sign.

Mars in Aquarius

Mars in Aquarius usually forges intense friendships that may or may not include sex. The thrusting, charge-ahead energy of the god of war is tempered when he is placed in Aquarius because Aquarius is about thinking and mental stimulation, not always about acting.

Expect surges of sexual heat with this sign. Mars in Aquarius may not be interested in having sex for weeks, and then will get on a roll and want you available now and for the next week. Then something else catches Mars in Aquarius's attention, and it's back to a sexual fast. The best way to encourage a more consistent flow of lovemaking is to talk about things that interest her. To start with the abstract and move to the physical is the only way to get to the person with Mars in Aquarius.

Written in the Stars
A wonderful gift for a person with either Mars or Venus in Aquarius would be jewelry with an aquamarine stone. The clear blue reminds these people of the limitless sky.

Venus in Aquarius

Venus in Aquarius denotes a very self-possessed person who may not need sex all the time, but when in the vicinity of a charming guy or girl, Venus in Aquarius is happy to let coolness go and see what happens. As with all Aquarian placements, there is an emphasis on friendly communication. Pats on the back, hugs, and hair tousles may be the subtle clues that a Venus in Aquarius person has that special tingle for you. He won't usually be in hot pursuit.

This placement is also not particularly modest or uptight about sexual relations. If it happens one night, fine. There may be another occasion, or the two of you can continue being friends. Men and women with this placement will pursue a very individual type of person. There are no hang-ups here about a relationship between people of very different ages.

Chapter 12

Pisces
(February 19–March 20)

Pisces, the last sign of the zodiac and the final water sign, lives between dreams and reality. In ancient times, jovial Jupiter ruled Pisces. With the discovery of Neptune in 1846, astrologers observed that the foggy, hazy, mysterious planet Neptune delineated the Piscean character more fully. Today, astrologers consider both Jupiter and Neptune as co-rulers of Pisces. The influence of Jupiterian good humor helps Pisces when oceans of emotions threaten to drown her. Her great strength and her great challenge are the same: feeling.

The Dreamer

The symbol of Pisces, two fish tied together, highlights her dual character: one fish is above the sea and living in the earth's atmosphere, and the other fish remains in the depths of the ocean. The underwater fish is the source of Pisces's dreamy, creative, and sexy nature. Sometimes, this underwater fish is unfathomable to even Pisces herself. In the realm of sex, she may not consciously know what she is doing, but her body and feelings do, and that makes her an alluring and extremely attractive partner. In terms of bedroom life, Pisces courts sex through attraction rather than pursuit. She loves to escape with her partner into a world removed from everyday cares. Whatever she does, you will never quite understand her, but why bother? Getting between the sheets with her sensitivities and gentle nature is more than good enough.

Written in the Stars

If Pisces listens to his very sensitive system, he will avoid overloading it with drinking and drugs because it usually feels bad and catches up with him in later years. Pisces aren't usually teetotalers, but they note the effects of stimulants and consciously choose whether they are worth the buzz.

The entire zodiac traces the development of the individual, as well as describing personality traits and sexual temperaments. We start with Aries and finish with

Pisces; each sign adds a different quality to the soul and personality. As the last sign of the zodiac, Pisces represents submerging the ego and leaping into the great ocean of the soul's freedom. It may sound heavy duty and metaphysical, but Pisces is not focused on earthly details. He dreams of a better world and is continually adjusting his expectations to the less-than-comfortable reality that surrounds him. Pisces wants to give his creativity and dreams of the world to another. He may have his egotistical moments, but deep down, Pisces really feels best in devotion and service to another. He gets off on doing what you would like and what you dream about.

The dream world of Pisces flourishes with an ocean of sexual possibilities that surround her. As a water sign, Pisces feels her way through the world. She catches the vibes between people and sends out the subtlest of signals when she wants to be caught or is fishing for someone.

What Turns Pisces On—and Off

Pisces is turned on by a strong lead. Pisces respond to partners who know they want. Pisces also don't mind being pushed in the direction of sex. Dominance scenarios and playing master or mistress and slave could be just the game to develop the best in Pisces's sexual nature.

Another turn-on is any kind of sensual enhancement: music, incense, candles, soft and nubby materials, a favorite pair of silk pajamas, or a love cocktail and special aphrodisiac. Pisces doesn't need stimulants to get her going, but she loves the ritual of preparing to move from the regular world into the dreamy world of sense and delight. If this takes a long time, Pisces is very content. Her sexual rhythm tends to be languorous because she is absorbing so many feelings on so many different levels.

Written in the Stars

It is definitely a turn-on for Pisces to make love with a fountain or waterfall in the background. But a really hot environment is a plush rug in front of a roaring fire. The coziness and heat trumps the soothing sounds of water. After all, Pisces has all the water he needs in his nature. With a roaring fire, he gains the element he lacks.

Other turn-ons are those related to taste. Pisces loves to combine sex and food. Try a honey massage and get totally sticky licking the honey off each other. Pisces doesn't care if he has to throw out the sheets. The deliciousness of the experience is more important than a few yards of cotton. Good wine also stimulates the senses and loosens the flow of sexy feelings.

As to turnoffs, Pisces does not like people who are flashy and ostentatious dressers on a day-to-day basis. He may appreciate a costume in the bedroom, such as feathers, a silk smoking jacket, thigh-high stockings, and boots, boots, and more boots, but on the street, he likes his partner to keep a low profile. Gaudy jewelry on women or men is a major turnoff. Underneath, underwear can be outrageous. Or perhaps Pisces was dreaming of a hot date that morning and forgot to put on underwear at all. Sexy underwear that emphasizes the butt is a major turn-on.

Pisces does not want to be rushed or scheduled into a sexual date. When sex just seems to happen, the Fish feels comfortable. When she gets too involved with her conscious mind, it shuts down her well of feeling. It is like the difference between the person who picks up dance steps by feeling and without words, and the person who has to mark out everything and be conscious of every muscle. Pisces wants the whole tango without worrying about an individual step or technique.

A partner who goes for sex without any preliminaries, foreplay, or romance is another major turnoff for Pisces. You have to first dip your feet in the water, get used to the temperature, splash a little, and then dive in for full immersion.

Pisces's Strengths and Specialties

If you want a considerate partner who may be content to sit on the couch and rub your feet for an evening, Pisces is the person for you. He is so sensitive—and can be turned on by the dimple in your cheek or the way a lock of hair falls over your eye—that a love affair with Pisces may be a continual sensual treat. His sensitivity makes him a master of cuddling and soft touching. Some signs have sex to relax, but Pisces likes to relax and then have sex.

Pisces enjoys oral sex a lot. She is very taste oriented, and any body part enhanced with honey, Marshmallow Fluff, or Nutella will drive her wild. The strongest sexual stimulant for Pisces is to join her fantasy with her physical senses; once that connection is made, there is no limit to sexual expression and satisfaction.

Pisces's Weaknesses and Foibles

Due to Pisces's extreme sensitivity, this sign is not a model of robust health. He is affected by changes in the weather, mood, and anything he eats or drinks that is not harmonious with his system. He frequently overindulges in liquor that leaves him weak and hung over.

But a mature Pisces knows how to take care of her physical and psychic health. She may be a lifelong shopper at the health-food store and take many vitamins to support her sensitive system. This type of mature Pisces will not only be a smooth and sexy partner, but also an example of how to combine clean living with awesome sex.

The Pisces rhythm is slow. Before a Pisces will have sex with anyone, he needs to feel out the situation. It is unusual for a Pisces to see, beckon, and have a sexual opportunity. The only exception to this is when he has had a wee bit too much to drink. If alcohol does not totally impair his sexual functioning, then under the influence, many unexpected things may happen.

Written in the Stars
Pisces will rarely confront a partner to improve the physical aspect between them. If sex is not working out, she will make a vague excuse about taking care of something and be gone. Pisces cannot easily verbally describe what she wants and needs. You will only know from her nonverbal communication.

A definite Pisces weakness is falling into the "blahs." This apathy may come upon him when he is stressed or just world weary. During these times, he is not very interested in sex or anything else and will just mope around. The best antidote for the Piscean blahs is to let him know that you need sex now, and that he is the only one who can help you out of your predicament. Pisces can respond to this call for help very well, and it will shake him out of the depths of whatever wallowing he may be indulging in.

The Pisces Man

If you love to dance before sex, this is the man for you. Pisces men have a wonderful sense of rhythm and music. He picks up the beat and goes with whatever melody is played. He is frequently found in the artistic and helping professions. In addition to working hard, he has acute perceptions about other people that can lead them toward success. The Pisces man is usually totally unconcerned about money. He may make it easily or not care if he has it at all. For him, there are more important parts of life to concentrate on.

In the bedroom, a Pisces man can be oblivious to anyone's agenda but his own. This can be positive in that he rarely criticizes a partner, but it also creates a tendency to be in love with love and to attract a partner who will not reciprocate his lust. Pisces then can be a martyr to his own sensitivity. When someone has caught his eye, even if totally inappropriate for him, he falls hard and recuperates slowly.

A Pisces man wants a partner who is organized, and does not mind a dominant personality. If his partner wants sex this way, that way, or any other way, he is happy to oblige. His needs usually are satisfied by careful prior selection. If the vibes aren't good, he won't even go near that person. The Pisces man is a family man and may not spend a lot of time playing the field before he makes a commitment. He is faithful and attentive because the pain of hurting someone he likes or loves is more than his sensitive nature can bear.

None of these descriptions mean that Pisces is wimpy. Water is a strong element, and like water, Pisces accomplishes his goal by applying steady pressure, and by wearing down the object of his desire with consistent attention and flow of feeling. It can be irresistible if you are caught up in the net of his charm.

After Libra, Pisces is the most romantic sign of the zodiac. The Pisces man likes dating rituals, enjoys long walks and sweet conversations, and never approaches sex in a direct way. When you get cozy with a Pisces man, he leads by touch and telepathy. You'll get the message and be delighted that you followed. It is a subtle lead and can be squashed by a partner who requires lots of explicit instructions or discussion. Talk with a potential Pisces partner on the phone, and it will take a minimum of fifteen minutes for the flow of feelings between you to settle in. After that, conversation is foreplay until you get together.

The Pisces Woman

The subtle appeal of a Pisces woman is that you may not be sure what she is doing, but you are more than willing to keep coming back for more. A Pisces woman will soothe her friends, and with her partners, her great sense of empathy intuits what part of their body needs touching and exactly how much pressure to apply.

She may prefer to dress in black and white and then go through a lavender phase. Frequently with Pisces women, there is an element of costume in their dress that suggests a historical time period. Lace and ruffles usually look good on her because she is a girly girl, even if she is the top internist in the hospital. Sexually, a Pisces woman gains pleasure from her partner's delight and orgasm. She wants pleasure also, but is so sensitive to all the feelings involved in merging sexually with another person that sometimes she gets hot just from handholding. A Pisces woman is hypersensitive, and when she abandons herself to feeling, you are talking about an ocean of possibilities.

Written in the Stars

All Pisces tend to be psychic, whether they are aware of it or not. When a Pisces woman meets someone, she knows intuitively whether the attraction will lead to sex or not. She may dance around the question for some time, but sooner or later, the Piscean charm and sympathetic vibrations will lasso her partner, and both will enjoy the result.

The Pisces woman needs to retreat from people and the world. She may periodically curl up in a ball and listen to music or watch old movies all night. This is protective and regenerative. If your Fish is in one of these periods, the only way to coax her out is cuddling and softness. Her juices will not respond to demands or overt passion. Baby talk might be exactly the right recipe. A Pisces woman retains a connection with her childhood sensitivity that makes her more compassionate and responsive to stimuli that other people offer. She needs to protect this part of her. Like all the water signs, she absorbs too many feelings and periodically must discharge them so they don't drag her down.

Once a Pisces woman is in bed, with curtains drawn and incense burning, she wants everything to flow smoothly. She wants romance and she wants effortless sex. Her hands speak, as do her thighs, her mouth, and her tongue. She usually doesn't talk because, with all her senses open, she does not want to get her mind going.

She can be sexually daring if the flow of physical feeling goes in that direction. She won't plan for a kinky scenario, but if it happens and feels right, why not? Pisces as the last sign of the zodiac understands all colors of the sexual palette.

The sense of touch in a Pisces woman is exquisitely sensitive. She is also open to stimulants of any kind to enhance pleasure. If you hear of an aphrodisiac from the Incas, the Pisces woman will probably know about it and have a bottle in her medicine cabinet.

Pisces women are susceptible to suggestion, which means that a whisper to step into the living room and examine the fluffy rug up close will get her going. She is not keen on less-than-private sex. But she will enjoy a romantic seduction in a public place that leads to you both running up the stairs to the bedroom.

Setting the Scene

Book a long weekend at a hidden lagoon where your room faces the water, and don't plan to come out until Monday morning. Travel with your own "Do Not Disturb" sign and alert room service before you arrive. A Pisces sex tryst needs a faraway feeling and a place that is utterly protected. From the moment you arrive, with candles, fresh fruit, and a bottle of champagne left in the room to welcome you, the atmosphere points to a pleasure harbor where Pisces unwinds and relaxes. The bed should have lots of pillows and a thick comforter if it is cold. An even better choice is a tropical setting that is warm and shady.

Pisces prefers the shadows, and all he needs for good sex is the mystery of two bodies touching in the dark. Nature and his feelings (because the vibes are so right) lead him to do whatever feels good. There is, of course, a Jacuzzi in this sexual hideout, or maybe a private sauna. Beautiful rugs cover the floor so that Pisces does not have to touch the floor with bare feet. Music comes from hidden speakers, and melodies are mixed with the sound of the surf and gentle rain falling. When Monday morning comes, you both will emerge from your retreat satisfied and refreshed.

Sexy Matches: The Hot and Not-So-Hot Combinations

Pisces's sensitivity may pick up a vibe with someone who is in a not-so-hot combo, and the relationship will work out just beautifully. Who knows? This could be a past-life partner who is perfect for Pisces this time around. This list of combinations is a guide, but it is always best for Pisces to follow her own intuitions.

Pisces and Aries

The last and first signs of the zodiac can be surprisingly good together in bed. Pisces oozes feeling and loves to lavish attention on Aries because Aries is so charming and vibrant. Pisces is not a competitive sign and does not challenge Aries. Pisces soothes Aries and that is a rest from the usual experience in which Aries participates. A Pisces should start at the Aries's feet and kiss all the way up to the head, pausing for special attention on the belly and navel.

The elements of Pisces and Aries are water and fire, and together they create steam heat. Over time, Aries's jumpy rhythm will wear on Pisces. There are not enough still, peaceful moments with the Ram for Pisces's sensitive taste. Pisces will turn to Aries for special-occasion sex, and then swim toward a less sexy, but easier combo.

Pisces and Taurus

Neptune and Venus together in the elements of water and earth are a fertile combination (in the baby-producing meaning, if applicable, as well as the sexy meaning). Pisces flows into Taurus's solid sensuality, and their rhythms are in sync. Both signs love comfort and enjoy creating an environment that cushions them from the outside world. The usual Piscean lack of concern for money and security may bug Taurus, but the pleasure of the Fish's company can calm the Bull's security concerns. This is a hot combo, with short- and long-term potential.

Pisces and Gemini

This is the astrological square relationship that challenges two people. Here, both signs are mutable, but they are in different elements, and the combo is not so hot because their rhythms are so different. Just about the time that Pisces is getting used to some sexual idea that Gemini proposes, Gemini is on to something else. This confuses Pisces and puts him in a tailspin. If

Pisces is the stronger in the relationship and Gemini follows his lead, these two will have some good times in the short term. Pisces drives Gemini wild with his all-knowing intuition, as Gemini has a more mental approach to life. When this translates into sex, the result is interesting and exotic, but not comfortable.

Pisces and Cancer

Water flows to water, and these two water signs are harmonious and a hot combo. Pisces and Cancer are psychically attuned, can tolerate the vagaries of each other's sensitivities, speak always in terms of feelings, and are not happy with crass reality. They may be better together for a long-term relationship. Neither sign enjoys one-night stands or a quick roll in the hay. They like to settle in with each other, and when this happens—and it's good—why bother to change?

Passion Points

Pisces rules the feet. Foot massage is probably the most sensual event in a Pisces's life. Lick the toes and kiss the arch. And if you can give him the gift of comfortable shoes, then you have a partner and grateful friend for life. Curiously, Pisces is not usually a foot fetishist. His fantasies are usually reserved for full-bodied sex in dreamy settings rather than getting aroused by one part of the body.

Pisces and Leo

Water and fire are the elements here, and the combo is not so hot. Pisces is too vague and willowy for robust, sunny Leo. The elusive Pisces is a never-attainable challenge for Leo, which can propel a sexual fling for a while, but the relationship sputters when Pisces cannot focus on Leo's need for individual attention. There are so many other people who need a Pisces's help and don't require such high maintenance. The area where these two meet is mutual generosity. If that feeling extends to the bedroom, there can be some hot sex for a while. If Pisces finds himself attracted to Leo, he should concentrate on the area between the feet and the small of the back, with lots of rubs and caresses.

Pisces and Virgo

These are opposite signs, with their elements of water and earth. Together, they are a hot combo for short- and long-term sex. Their elements harmonize, but the real kicker between the two of them is that Pisces's hazy, Neptunian view of the world relaxes Virgo's detail-oriented, analytical mind. Somehow when they are together, each feels that the other has taken care of things, and this frees them to enjoy each other. Sexually, they create a world of their own. A Pisces should concentrate on the left shoulder and back of the neck of a Virgo, with, of course, some sweet attention to the feet.

Pisces and Libra

These two romantic signs make for good sex in the short term. The ruling planets here are Neptune and Venus, and the phrase "looking at the world through rose-colored glasses" describes perfectly the charm of Libra and Pisces together. They are masters of foreplay and wooing, and they have so much sensitivity that sexually things unfold very well. Both signs tend to be slightly passive with sex, so they may get trapped in an "after you" scenario, but there is enough sexual juice between them to figure this one out without conflict. Neither sign handles anger or conflict well. Since both signs have trouble with decisions long term, the relationship may flounder, but in the trying-out phase, there is a lot of pleasure.

Pisces and Scorpio

The fact that these are two water elements in a trine relationship means oceans of pleasure. These signs together are hot, and not only because of Scorpio's famous reputation as a sexual superpower. Pisces is the only sign that Scorpio cannot control. The Fish slips away, refuses to engage in power struggles, and then comes back and surprises Scorpio with let's-make-up sex that knocks her off her feet. The planets are Neptune and Mars, and there is a touch of divine madness in this combination that will keep both partners connected and intrigued for a long time. Pisces will go along with anything Scorpio proposes and may feel liberated to try a few personal fantasies. Together, they are good for the short and long term, and everything in between.

Pisces and Sagittarius

The elements here of water and fire are usually not so hot, as they form a square relationship. However, remember that Pisces used to have Sag's ruler, Jupiter. The abundance and expansive nature of both signs magnify their sexual chemistry when they come together. Pisces will have to get used to Sag's brusqueness and large sexual appetite, but she is up to the challenge. Also, Pisces and Sag like to concentrate on the same areas of the body: the legs and feet. Use this information as a prelude to exploring more intimate areas, and this combo can be hot.

Pisces and Capricorn

The Fish and the Goat are hot together. Capricorn may be the more lustful sign, but Pisces is the water element and easily stimulates Capricorn's lust. There are opportunities here for pleasure and commitment. Both signs are good kissers, and with the added dimension of Pisces's extrasensory perception, together these two can reach the heights of physical pleasure.

Pisces and Aquarius

These are next-door-neighbor signs in water and air, and at base are not so hot. They live in different universes, and Pisces is too vague for electrified Aquarius. The quality of their sexual energy is also very different. Pisces is diffuse, and Aquarius is supercharged. Having sex once or twice when all the lights are off at the after-hours club may be an adventure for Pisces's scrapbook, but a regular diet of this irregular combo probably won't work out.

Pisces and Pisces

Flow and more flow happens between the four fish! Pisces has the urge to merge with a sexual partner because it makes her feel connected and less alone. This means anything goes sexually because the feeling of being taken over by sensation is the major turn-on. When sex is between two mature Pisces, there is harmony and pleasure in abundance. Both Pisces have learned how to manage their sensitivity as well as the demands of the world, and sexually, they just relax and let go. If, however, the two Pisces in question are immature and swimming in a world of escapist pleasure, this can be double trouble. Pisces and Pisces become so involved in escaping from the world that no one pays the rent, and then their pleasure palace will evaporate.

Sex Planets: Mars and Venus

To refine your knowledge of how the sign Pisces manifests in Mars and Venus, read the following descriptions. Pisces is always a subtle vibration, and knowing if your partner's or your own Mars or Venus is in Pisces can clue you in to many different aspects of a sexual personality.

Mars in Pisces

As you know, Mars is the god of war. What happens when the god of war is affiliated with the hazy, dreamy planet, Neptune? The answer is, "Not much." Neptune says, "Let's not fight, let's not challenge anyone; let's build our communication on spiritual and loving principles; and if we still can't get along, let's just have a drink and forget all the Sturm und Drang." Mars's assertive energy is not easily expressed when he is in dreamy Pisces. People with this placement can succeed when they are involved with the helping professions. As partners, Mars in Pisces is so considerate and tender that you may want to encourage a more go-get-'em approach. Yet this sign has a strong sex drive; he just goes about fulfilling it in a very subtle way. Mars in Pisces is idealistic and wants sex to be part of a relationship, however brief it may be. Sharing your dreams during sex may be the greatest turn-on for Mars in Pisces. Mars in Pisces is very mindful of his partner's pleasure as well as his own.

Venus in Pisces

Venus in Pisces is astrologically considered to be an exalted position. The yielding nature of Venus fits very well with Piscean compassion and sensitivity. This is the position of great friendship and kindness. And if that friendship includes sex, Venus in Pisces is happy to oblige.

Written in the Stars

Amethyst is the stone for Pisces in general, and anyone with Venus in Pisces would love such a gift.

People with this position usually are musically talented. Playing music or dancing will always enhance her love life.

One of the reasons that Venus is considered well placed in Pisces is because the erotic love that Venus represents is heightened by the universal love that Neptune, Pisces's planet, represents. In terms of sex, this means that not only will you have a good time, but also the experience could be divine and awaken all sorts of pleasure centers that you didn't know that you had.

Index

About the Author

Constance Stellas is an astrologer of Greek heritage with more than twenty-five years of experience. She primarily practices in New York City and counsels a variety of clients, including business CEOs, artists, and scholars. She has been interviewed by *The New York Times*, *Marie Claire*, and *Working Woman*, and appeared on several New York TV morning shows and national radio programs. Constance is the astrologer for *HuffPost*, and a regular contributor to Thrive Global. She is also the author of several titles, including *The Astrology Gift Guide*, *Advanced Astrology for Life*, *The Everything® Sex Signs Book*, and the graphic novel series Tree of Keys, as well as coauthor of *The Hidden Power of Everyday Things*. Learn more about Constance at her website, ConstanceStellas.com, or on *Twitter* (@Stellastarguide).